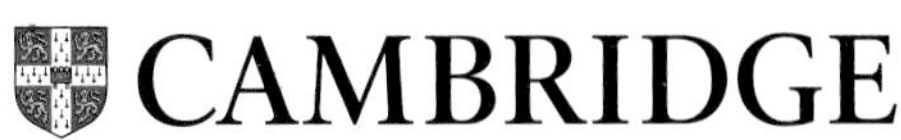

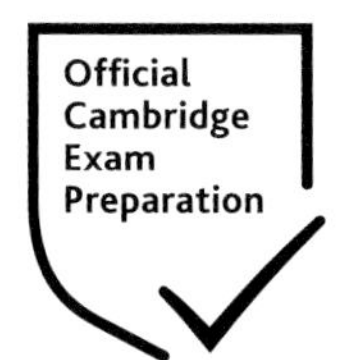

CAMBRIDGE

Official Cambridge Exam Preparation

Fun Skills

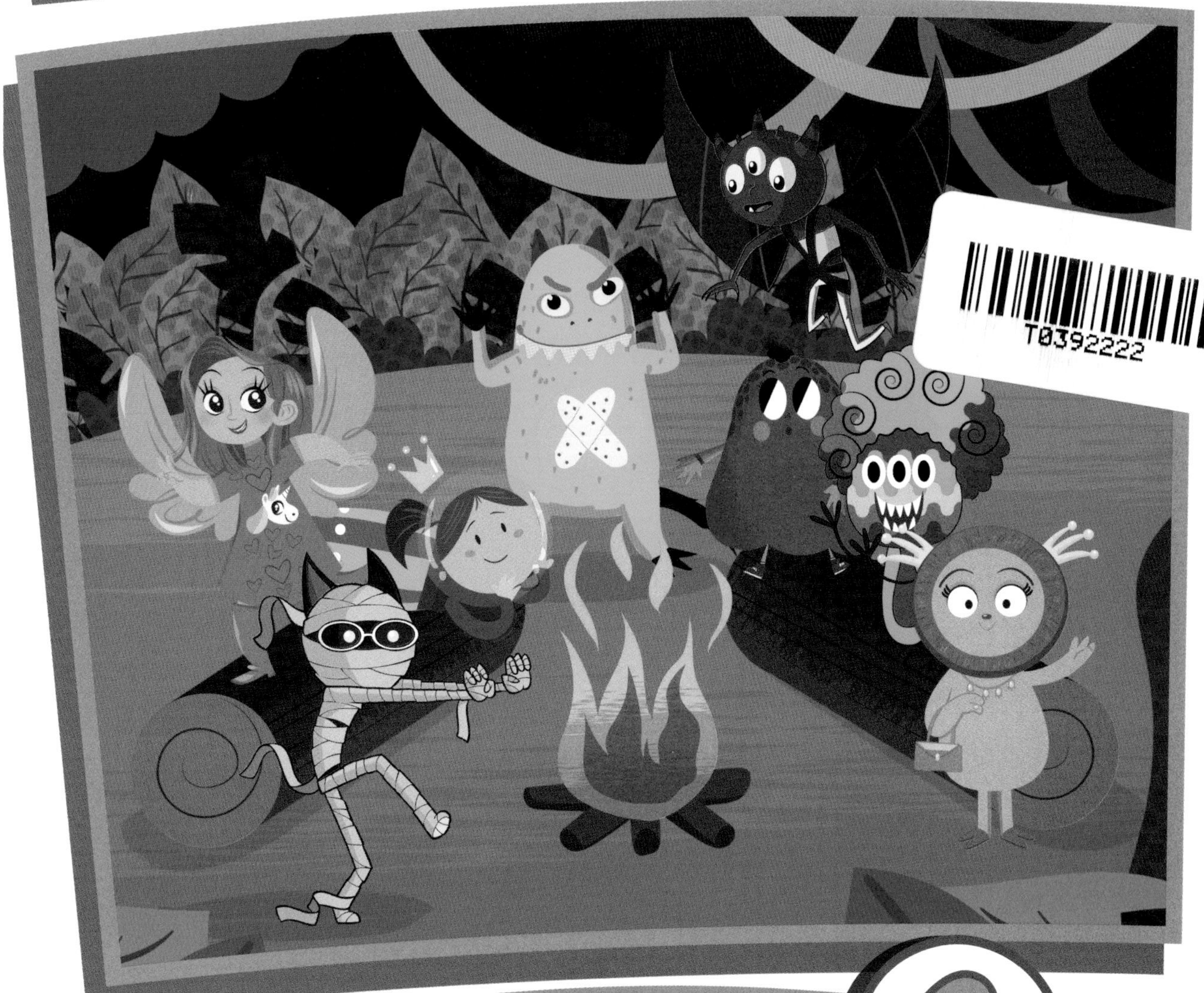

Student's Book 2

Claire Medwell • Montse Watkin

Cambridge University Press
www.cambridge.org/elt

Cambridge Assessment English
www.cambridgeenglish.org

Information on this title: www.cambridge.org/9781108673013

First published 2020

20 19 18 17 16 15 14 13 12 11 10 9 8 7

Printed in Malaysia by Vivar Printing

A catalogue record for this publication is available from the British Library

ISBN 978-1-108-67301-3 Student's Book and Home Booklet with Online Activities

Contents

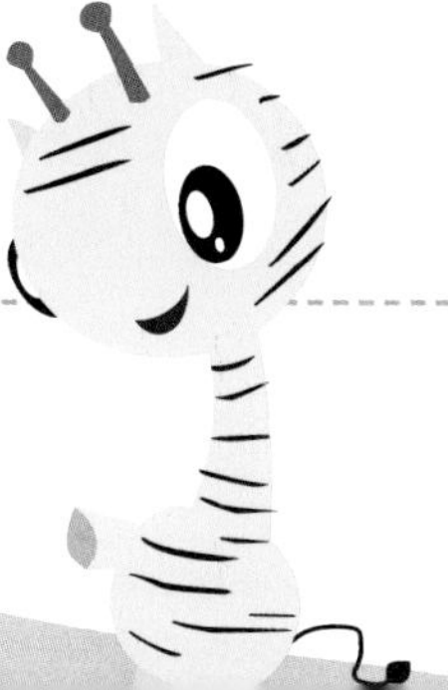

Map of the book

Unit	Topic	Skills focus	Can do	
1 My school bag page 6	School bags and contents	**Reading and Writing** Read short sentences and recognise key words Tick or cross to show if a sentence is true or false	Read and understand short, simple words and the names of familiar objects	Chant Think Big
2 Fun in the park! page 10	Leisure activities	**Reading and Writing** Read short sentences about a picture and say whether they are true or not	Understand basic descriptions of everyday activities	
Review Units 1–2 *page 14*				
3 It's my birthday! page 16	Birthday activities Prepositions of place	**Listening** Identify key words in descriptions of people and select the correct name for each person by drawing a line to connect them **Speaking** Give and respond to simple instructions using prepositions of place	Understand simple spoken descriptions Understand and follow spoken instructions to point at and place objects in a picture	Chant
4 My favourite things page 20	Favourite things	**Reading and Writing** Spell simple words correctly **Speaking** Respond to simple questions	Unjumble words to match a picture Answer questions with simple answers and respond to *Tell me about …* questions	Chant
Review Units 3–4 *page 24*				
5 Let's go shopping! page 26	Things you can buy	**Listening** Listen for and write numbers (1–20) Spell names	Understand and write letters of the alphabet when heard Understand and write numbers 1–20 when heard	Song Think Big
6 Cool homes page 30	Houses, rooms and furniture	**Reading and Writing** Read a text, then choose and copy words to complete sentences	Understand and copy simple words	Think Big
Review Units 5–6 *page 34*				

1 My school bag

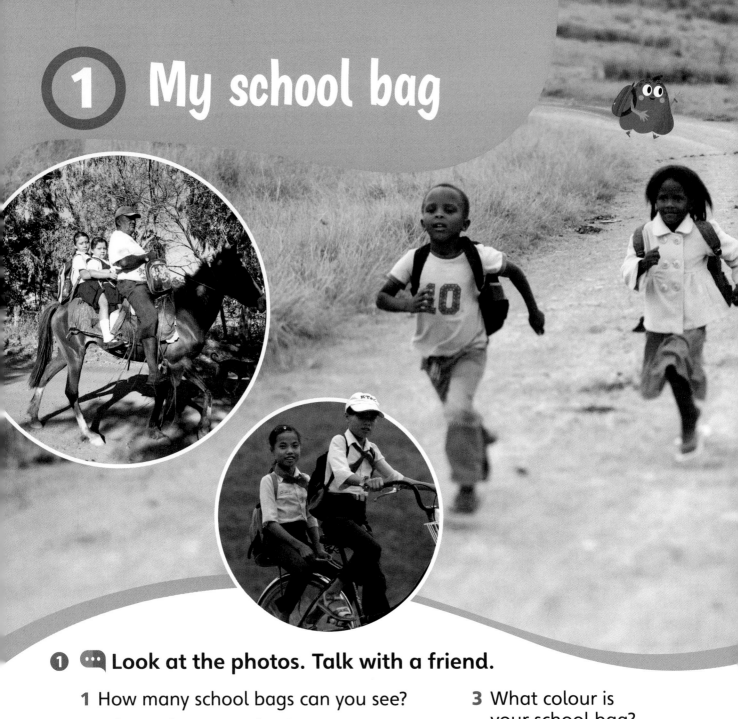

1 Look at the photos. Talk with a friend.

1 How many school bags can you see?
2 What colours are they?
3 What colour is your school bag?

2 02 Listen and match the bags to the children.

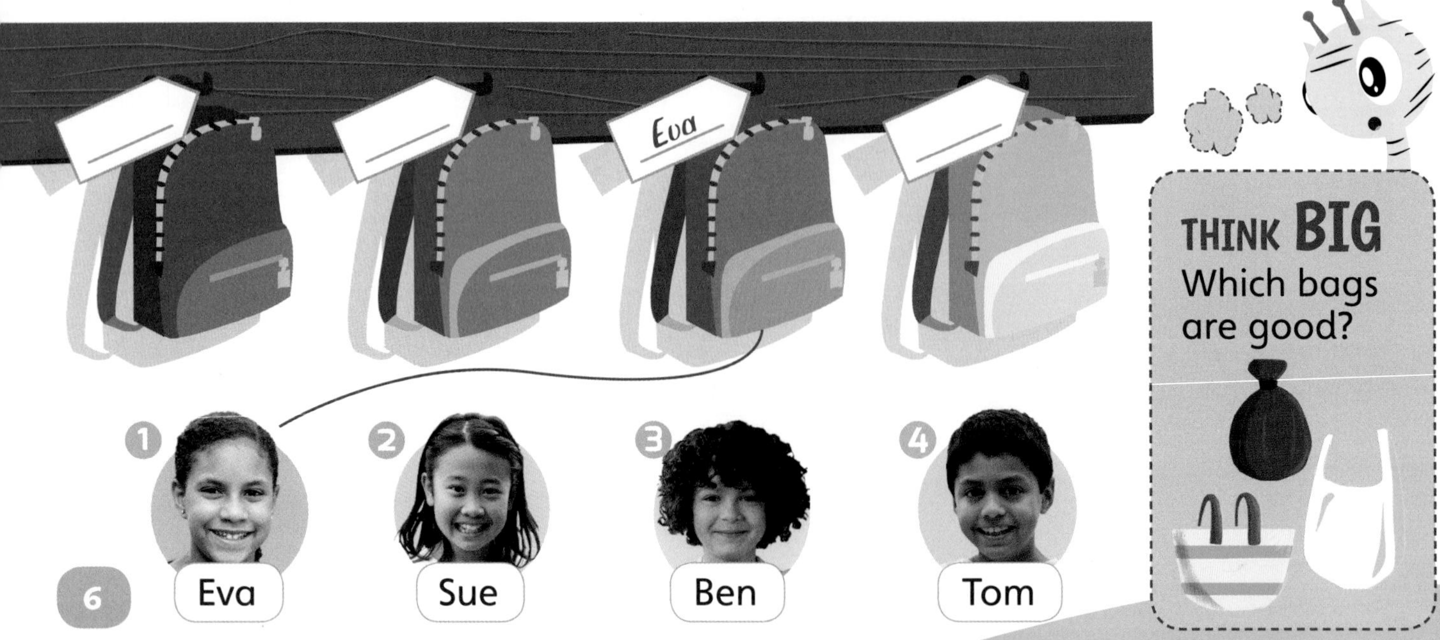

❸ Look at Max's school bag. How many things can you name?

❹ Draw three objects in your bag and write.

I've got ______________________ , ______________________

and ______________________ in my school bag.

❺ Find out about your friend's bag.

What's in your bag?

I've got a ruler.

Me too!

❻ Read, think and write.

1 ✓ It's in Max's bag. ✗ It's not in my bag.
It's ______________________ .

2 ✓ It's in my bag. ✗ It's not in Max's bag.
It's ______________________ .

3 ✗ It's not in my bag. ✗ It's not in Max's bag.
It's ______________________ .

1 Look at the photos. Talk with a friend.

What's this?

What are these?

It's a/an ...

They're ...

A

B

C

D

1 Be nice to wildlife.

2

3

4

Let's tidy up!

2 03 Listen to the chant and match the photos.

3 Complete the words.

Example post _e_ _r_

1 _ _ _ board

2 book _ _ _ _

3 _ _ _ puter

4 key _ _ _ _ _

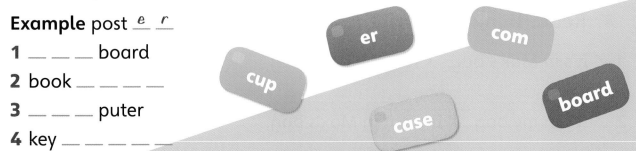

er com cup board case

4 Work with a friend. Give instructions and tidy your classroom.

TIP!

Don't forget to say *please* and *thank you*!

5 Look and read. Put a tick (✓) or a cross (✗) in the box. There are two examples.

Examples

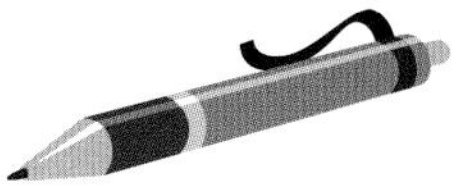

This is a pen. ✓

These are rulers. ✗

Questions

1  These are desks. ☐

2  This is a cupboard. ☐

3  This is a bookcase. ☐

4  These are crayons. ☐

5 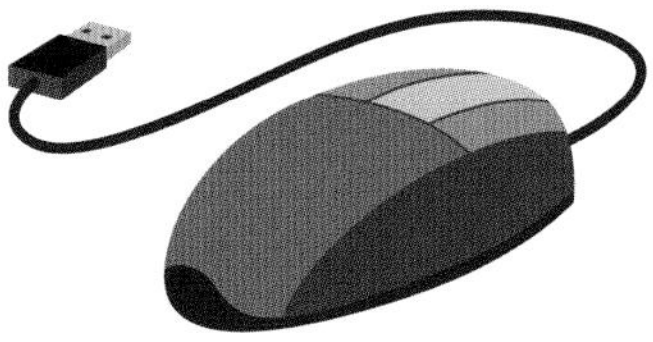 This is a poster. ☐

2 Fun in the park!

1 Look at the park for 30 seconds. What can you see?

2 Cover the picture and work with a friend. How many questions can you answer?

1 What colour are the bikes?
2 What animals are there?
3 How many children are there?
4 Where is the kite?
5 What sports can you see?
6 What's in the water?
7 What has the monkey got?
8 What is Frankie eating?

3 04 Listen and circle the word you hear.

1 see	(bee)	3	bike	kite	5	dogs	ducks
2 sun	fun	4	boat	boots	6	bat	bag

4 Match the children to the verbs.

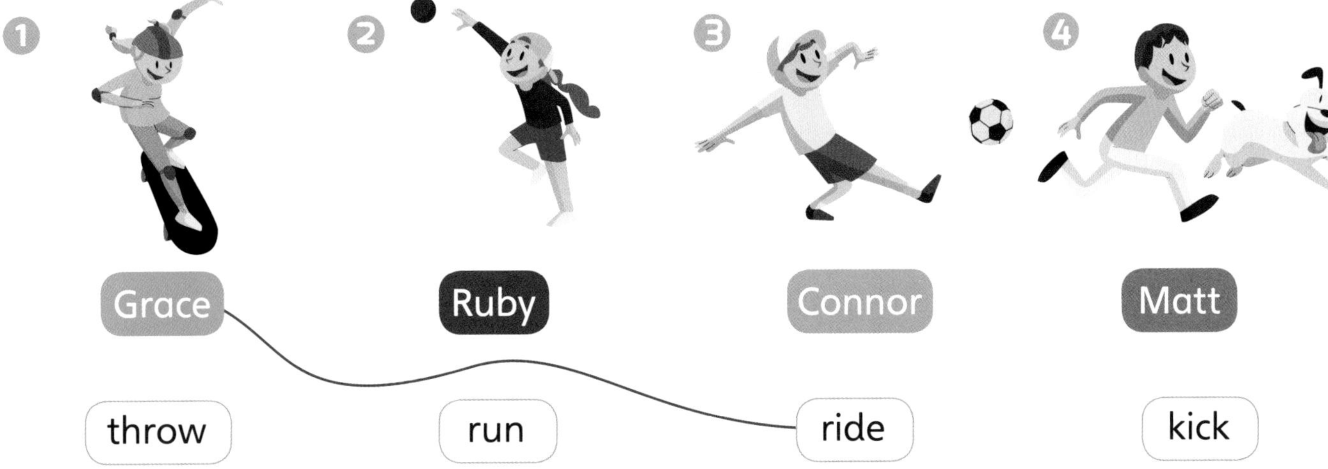

5 Look at the pictures in task 4. Listen and answer.

6 Write correct sentences.

Example Grace is holding her skateboard.

No, she isn't. She's *riding her skateboard*.

1 Matt is walking with his dog.

No, he isn't. He's ______.

2 Ruby is hitting a ball.

No, ______.

3 Connor is catching a football.

No, ______.

7 Imagine you are at the park. Do a mime. Can your friends guess?

1 Look at the park. Talk with a friend.

1 How many animals can you see?
2 What are the animals doing?

2 Look and read. Write *yes* or *no*.

Example A girl is walking with her dog. *yes*

1 The snake is holding an ice cream. ______
2 The crocodile is riding a bike. ______
3 The fish are sleeping in the water. ______
4 Grandpa has got a camera. ______
5 The monkey is flying a kite. ______

3 What's in the photos? Find and write the words.

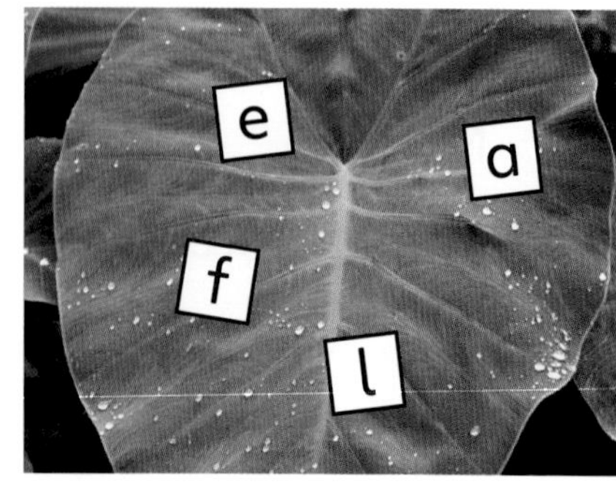

1 *t* _ _ _ 2 _ _ _ _ _ _ _ 3 _ _ _ _

4 Read and choose the correct words.

Enjoy a dirty / clean park.
Throw / Don't throw
your rubbish in the bin!
rubbish
bin

5 What is good? Choose the correct picture.

A 

B 

C 

6 Read the signs and match to the children in task 5. Write A, B or C.

1 ☐ 

2 ☐ 

3 ☐ 

7 Make a word tree!

Look at page 66.

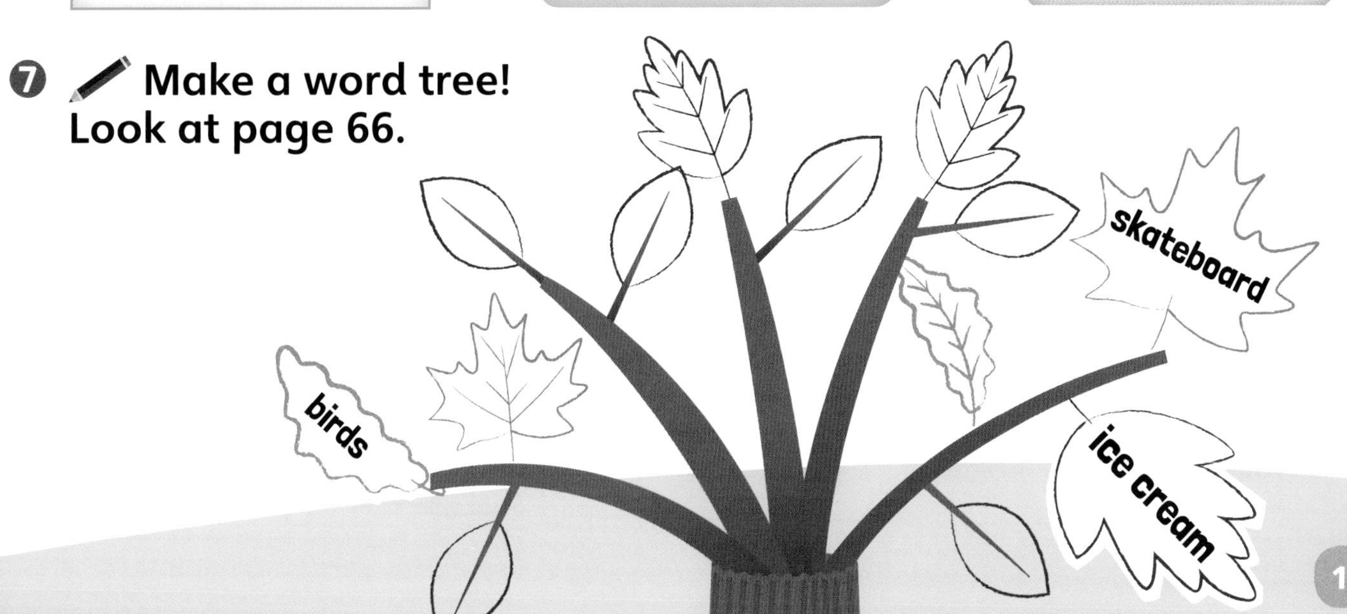

Review Unit 1

Skills: Speaking, Writing and Reading

1 Talk with a friend. Look at the photo and answer the questions.

1 Where are the children?

2 Name four things you see in this classroom.

3 Name four things you don't see.

Mark: ___ / 9

2 Look at the photos and write the words.

1 Eva's bag is ___orange___. It's in the ___________.

2 Ben's bag is ___________. It's on the ___________.

3 Sue's bag is ___________. It's next to the ___________.

Mark: ___ / 5

3 Read and draw the things.

Example

a football in the bookcase

1 a computer on the desk

2 a mouse next to the computer

3 a ruler in the school bag

4 a clock on the bookcase

5 three crayons on the chair

Mark: ___ / 5

Total: ___ ___ / 19

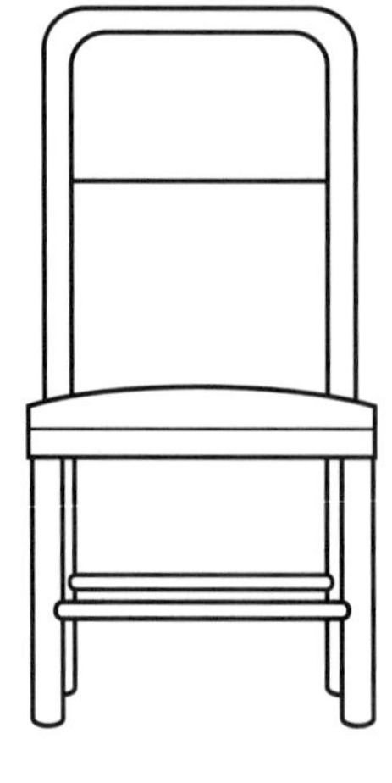

Skills: Reading and Writing

1 Look at the photos. Write these words on the lines.

~~hit~~ kick ride run

1 

2 

3 

4 

1 *hit* 2 ______ 3 ______ 4 ______

Mark: __ / 3

2 Look at the pictures and read the sentences. Write A or B.

A 

B

1 A girl is riding a bike. *A*
2 A boy is catching a basketball. __
3 A teacher is running. __
4 Two ducks are swimming. __
5 A dog is jumping. __
6 A girl is throwing a toy. __
7 A boy is flying a kite. __
8 A girl is kicking a football. __

Mark: __ / 7

3 Look at the colours and write Frankie's sentences.

1	ball	window.	Don't	the	next to	the	kick
	Don't		____		____	____	____ .
2	your	on	Don't	bike	grass.	ride	the
	____		____	____	____	____	____ .

Mark: __ / 6

Total: __ __ / 16

3 It's my birthday!

1 Read and point to the photos.

A get a special card
B open presents
C play party games
D wear new clothes
E sing a song
F eat special food

2 Talk with two friends. What do you do on your birthday?

I wear new clothes.

So do I!

I don't!

7

8

3 Can you guess what the presents are? Write the words.

1 k i t e

2 b _ _ _

3 r _ _ _ _

4 t _ _ _ _ b _ _ _

5 l _ _ _ _

6 b _ _ _

4 06 Where are the presents? Listen and draw lines.

5 Draw a toy on a small sticky note. Look at the picture in task 3. Give instructions to your friend.

Put the robot in front of the chair!

between | under | next to | behind | in front of

1 07 Listen to the chant and draw lines.

1
2
3
4
Sara
Dan
Lucy
Tom

2 08 Listen and circle the correct words.

1 **She's / Her** name's Sara. **She's / Her** nine years old.

2 **He's / His** name's Dan. **He's / His** seven years old.

3 Ask and answer with a friend.

How old are you?

What's her name?

How old is he?

4 Draw and write about you and your friend.

This is ME!
My name's
_______________.
I'm _______________
years old.
This is my friend.
____
_______________.
____
years old.

5 Look at the picture of a birthday party. What can you see?

6 09 Listen and draw lines. There is one example.

Anna Bill Kim Eva

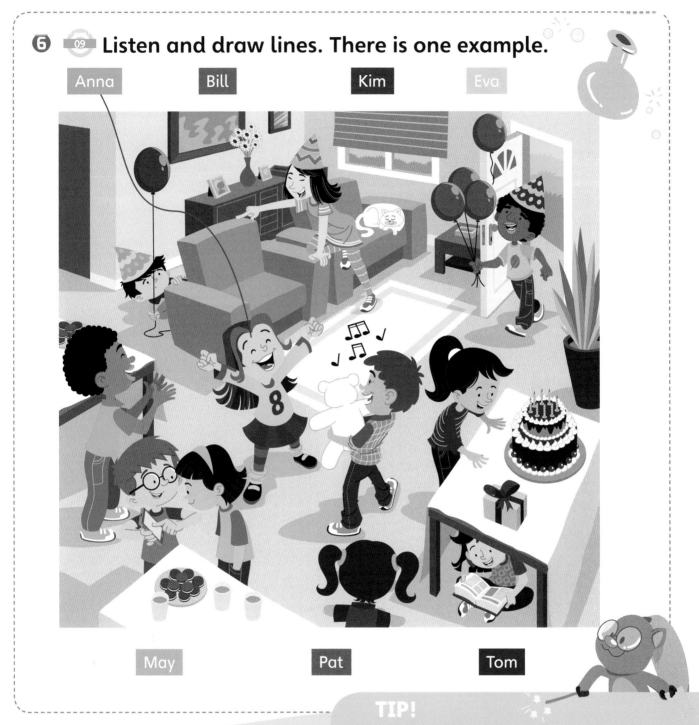

May Pat Tom

TIP!

There is one extra name. What is it?

7 Make a pop-up birthday card! Look at page 67.

4 My favourite things

1 10 **Find and write Nedda's favourite things. Then listen and check.**

My favourite …

colour rhymes with **new**.	*blue*
animal rhymes with **frog**.	______
toy rhymes with **white**.	______
food rhymes with **snake**.	______
place rhymes with **tree**.	______

2 **Read the groups of words. Circle the word that is not correct.**

1	2	3	4	5
colour	animal	toy	food	place
brown	giraffe	bread	pea	pink
(bear)	goat	board game	pear	park
black	grapes	ball	paper	playground

3 **Ask a friend about their favourite things.**

What's your favourite colour?
It's blue.

TIP!
Use only the letters in the hearts.

4 Look at the pictures. Look at the letters. Write the words.

Example

m a n g o

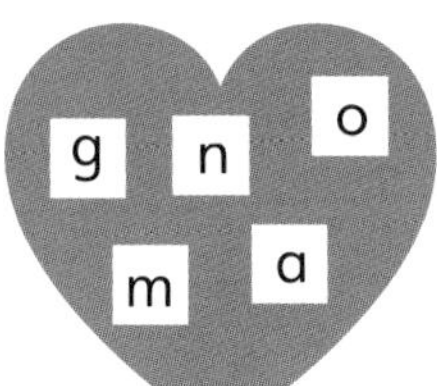

Questions

1 

_ _ _ _ _

4 

_ _ _ _ _ _

2 

_ _ _ _ _

5 

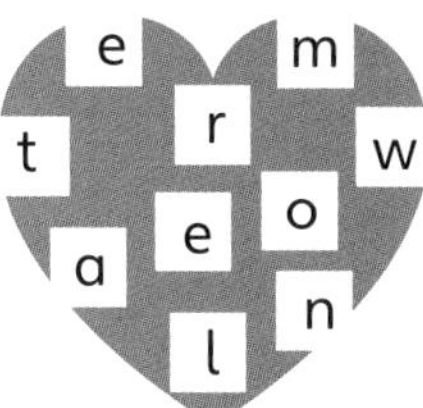

_ _ _ _ _ _ _ _ _ _

3 

_ _ _ _ _

5 Read and draw.

1 sweets on the cake

2 five peas on the ice cream

3 lemon in the lemonade

4 a monster in the story book

6 11 Listen to the chant. Draw the faces in task 5.

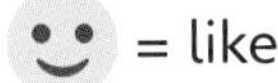 = like  = don't like

1 Look and write the words. Write one more question.

		Me	My frien
	1 Do you like p _ _ _ _ _ _ _ _ _ on your pizza?		
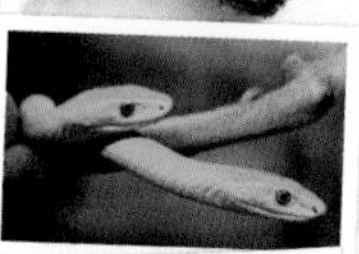	2 Do you like big s _ _ _ _ _ at the zoo?		
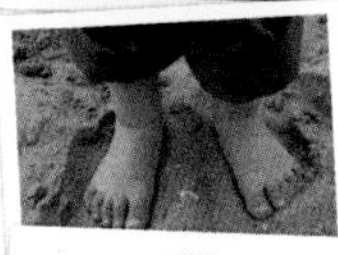	3 Do you like s _ _ _ under your feet?		
	4 Do you like f _ _ _ _ _ _ _ on TV?		
	5 ______________________________?		

Yes, I do! =  No, I don't! =

2 Ask and answer with a friend. Draw the faces in task 1.

3 Talk about the picture with a friend. Take turns to ask.

1 What's this?
2 Where is the alien?
3 What colour are the alien's eyes?
4 How many birds are there?
5 What is the alien doing?
6 Tell me about the lizard.

TIP! It's OK to say: *Sorry, I don't understand. Can you say that again, please?*

4 (12) **Listen to the interview and circle the correct information.**

1 The alien **likes / doesn't like** monsters.
2 The alien **likes / doesn't like** the sun.
3 Its favourite food is peas on **pizza / ice cream**.
4 The alien's favourite hobby is **flying / painting**.
5 It **likes / doesn't like** pink.

5 **Draw and write about an alien.**

My alien's name is ______________________ .

My alien has got ______________________

______________________ .

My alien lives ______________________

______________________ .

My alien likes ______________________

______________________ .

My alien doesn't like ______________________

______________________ .

6 **Show your alien to your friends.**

My alien's name is Zak.
What a cool alien!
Thanks!
What beautiful colours!

Review Unit 3

Skills: Speaking, Writing and Reading

1 **Look at the photos and talk with a friend. What can you see? What are the children doing?**

Mark: ___ / 4

2 **Read the text. Write these words on the lines.**

games He Her ~~my~~ eight too

Hi, I'm Sam! This is ___*my*___ friend, Bill. Bill is six years old. **1** ______ has got a sister. **2** ______ name is Suzi. She's **3** ______ years old. On Bill's birthday, we play **4** ______ and eat cake. We sing Happy Birthday! Bill likes birthdays. Me **5** ______ !

Mark: ___ / 5

3 **Look at the picture. Choose the correct word.**

Example The car is **in front of** / **next to** the robot.

1 The teddy bear is **next to** / **on** the table.

2 The cakes are **next to** / **in front of** the teddy bear.

3 The boy is **between** / **behind** the girls.

4 The toys are **under** / **on** the table.

5 The cat is **between** / **behind** the guitar.

Mark: ___ / 5

Total: ___ / 14

Skills: Listening, Writing and Reading

1 13 **What are Lucy's favourite things? Listen and circle.**

A 

B 

C 

D 

E 

F 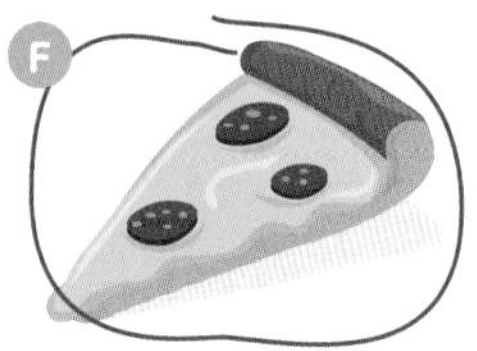

G 

H 

Mark: ___ / 4

2 **Now write about Nick.**

1 Nick's favourite animals are l i z a r d s
and _ _ _ _ _ _ _ _ _ .
2 Nick doesn't like pizza. His favourite food is a _ _ _ _ _ _ _ _ _ _ .
3 His favourite place is the _ _ _ _ _ _ _ _ _ .
4 Nick has a red _ _ _ _ _ _ _ _ . He plays with it in the park.
5 What is Nick's favourite colour? Yes, that's right, it's _ _ _ _ _ _ _ _ _ _ .

Mark: ___ / 5

3 **Look at the picture and read the questions. Circle the correct answer.**

Example What animal is in the sea? a fish / a lizard
1 What colour is the bird in the tree? green / purple
2 How many children are there? two / three
3 What is the boy wearing? boots / a hat
4 What is he holding? a boat / a fish
5 What is the girl doing? jumping / swimming

Mark: ___ / 5

Total: ___ / 14

5 Let's go shopping!

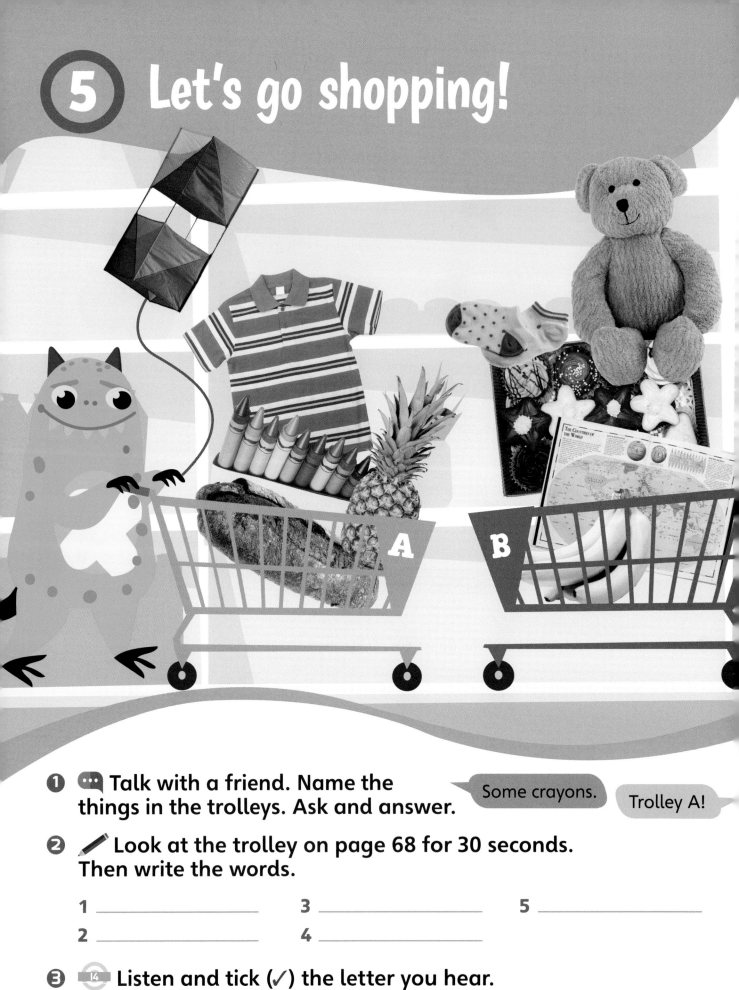

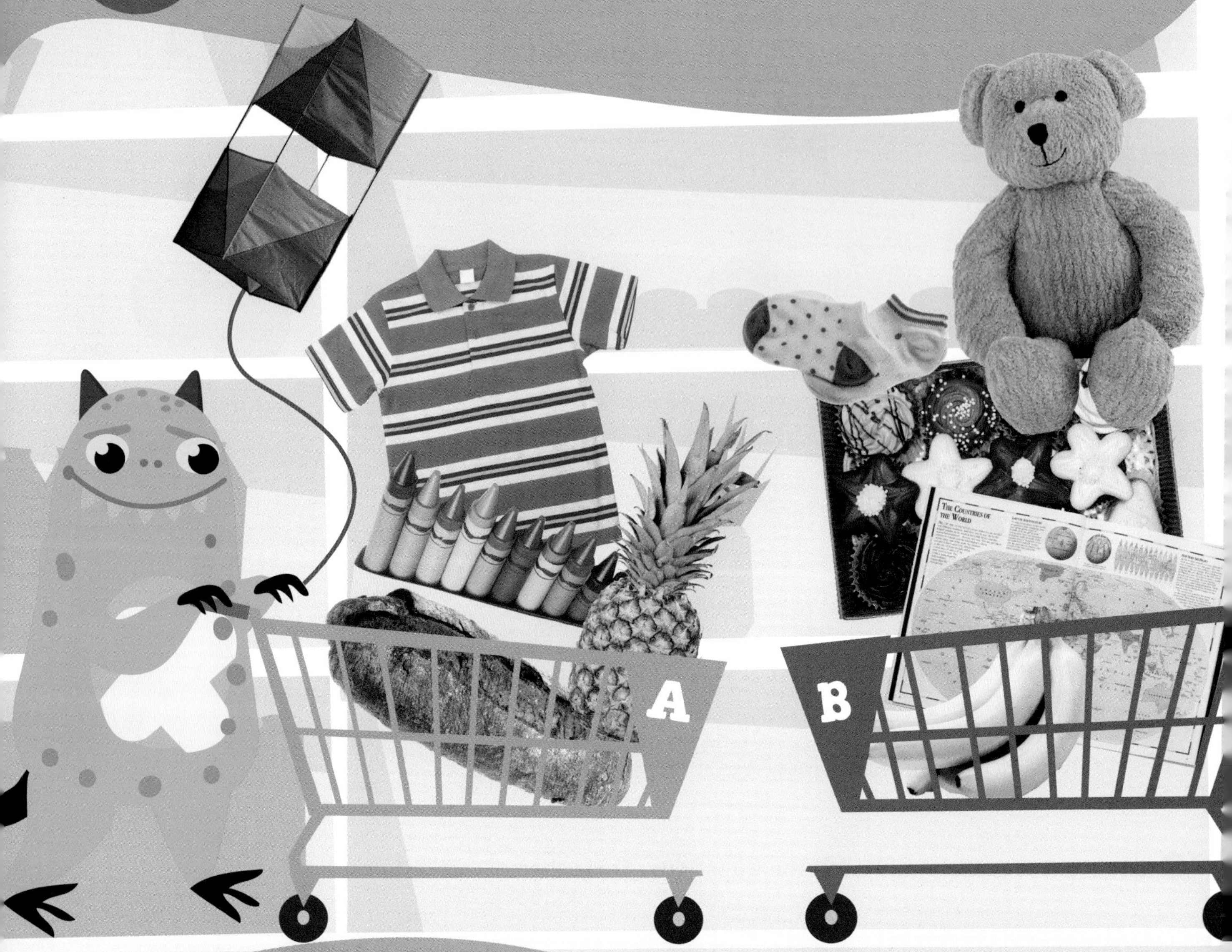

A

B

1 Talk with a friend. Name the things in the trolleys. Ask and answer.

Some crayons.

Trolley A!

2 Look at the trolley on page 68 for 30 seconds. Then write the words.

1 ________ 3 ________ 5 ________

2 ________ 4 ________

3 14 Listen and tick (✓) the letter you hear.

4 Write the first letters. Are the letters the same as in task 3?

_d_ olls

__ ineapples

__ ats

__ ce cream

__ ish

__ eans

__ eatballs

__ oots

5 Student A: Look at task 4. Ask three questions. Student B: Close your book and write.

Can you spell ...?

How do you spell ...?

6 15 Listen and write the surnames.

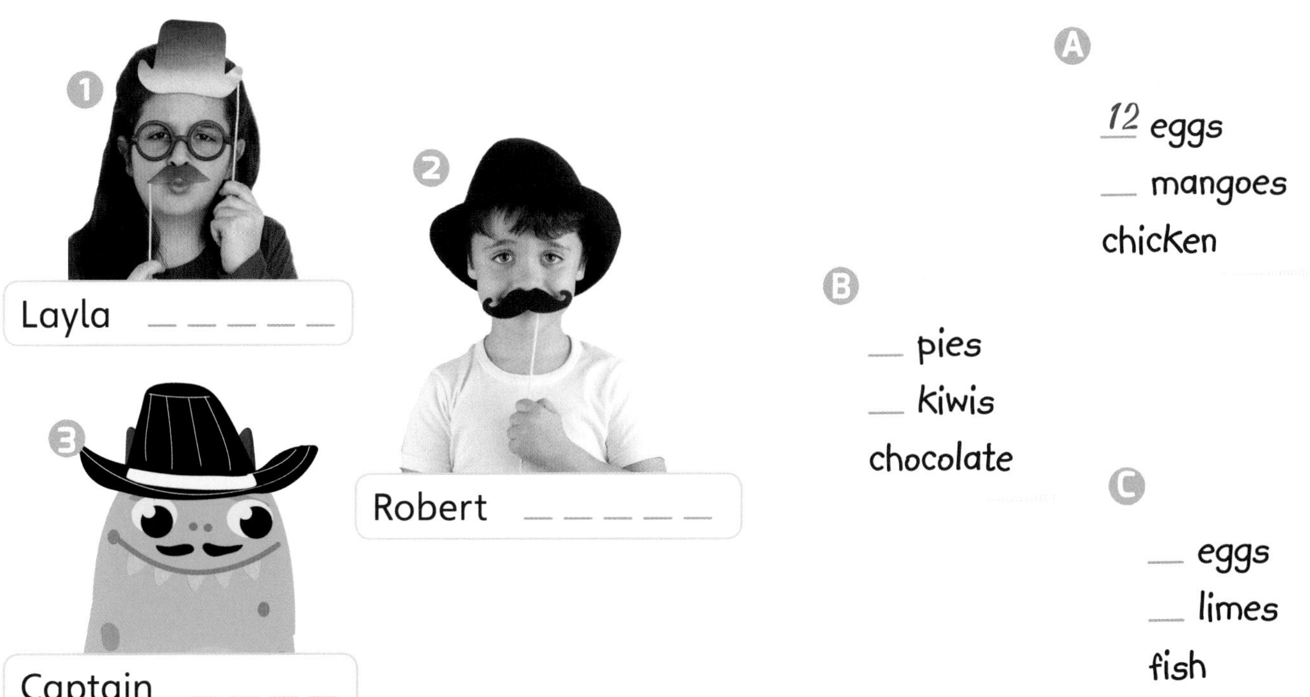

7 15 Listen again. Match the people to the shopping lists. Write the numbers in the shopping lists.

1 Listen to the song and do the maths. How many sunflowers are in the flower shop?

20	–	5	=	
15	–		=	
	–		=	
	–		=	

2 Complete your shopping list. Draw and write.

w _ _ _ _ _ _ _ _ _

____

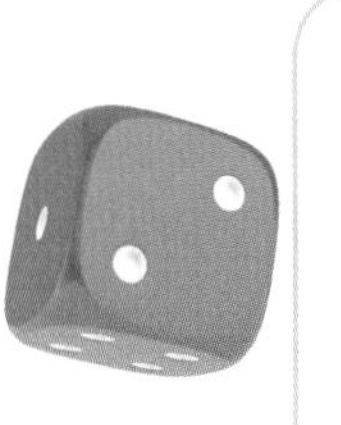

____

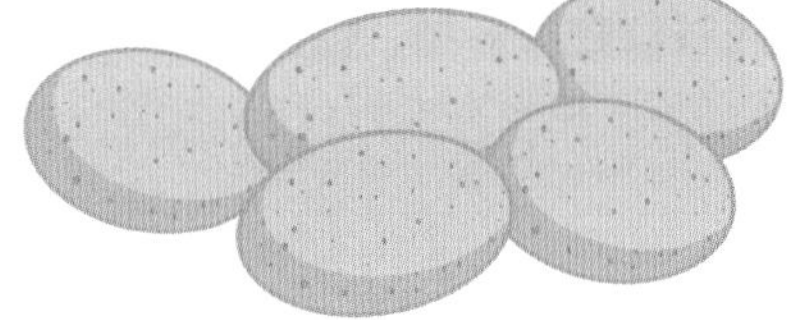

p _ _ _ _ _ _ _

t _ _ _ _ _ _ _

____

3 Play with a friend. Who can buy the things first?

I'd like a watermelon, please.

Here you are.

Can I have three tomatoes, please?

4 Read and point. Write the words.

We see numbers:

1 on a _ _ _ _ _ in our classroom. (k o c c l)

2 in a clothes _ _ _ _ . (h o s p)

3 on a _ _ _ in the street. (s u b)

4 on a birthday _ _ _ _ . (c e a k)

5 on the _ _ _ _ of a house. (o d o r)

THINK BIG

Where do you see numbers?

1

2

£10

3

Stocking Avenue via City Centre 15

4

5

5 Read the questions in task 6. Say *name* or *number*.

6 17 Read the question. Listen and write a name or a number. There are two examples.

Examples

What is the boy's name? Nick

How old is he? 9

Questions

1 What is the name of the street? ________ Street

2 What number is the shop? ________

3 Who is in the shop? Mrs ________

4 How many flowers does the girl want? ________

5 Who are the flowers for? ________

TIP!

All the answers are names or numbers.

6 Cool homes

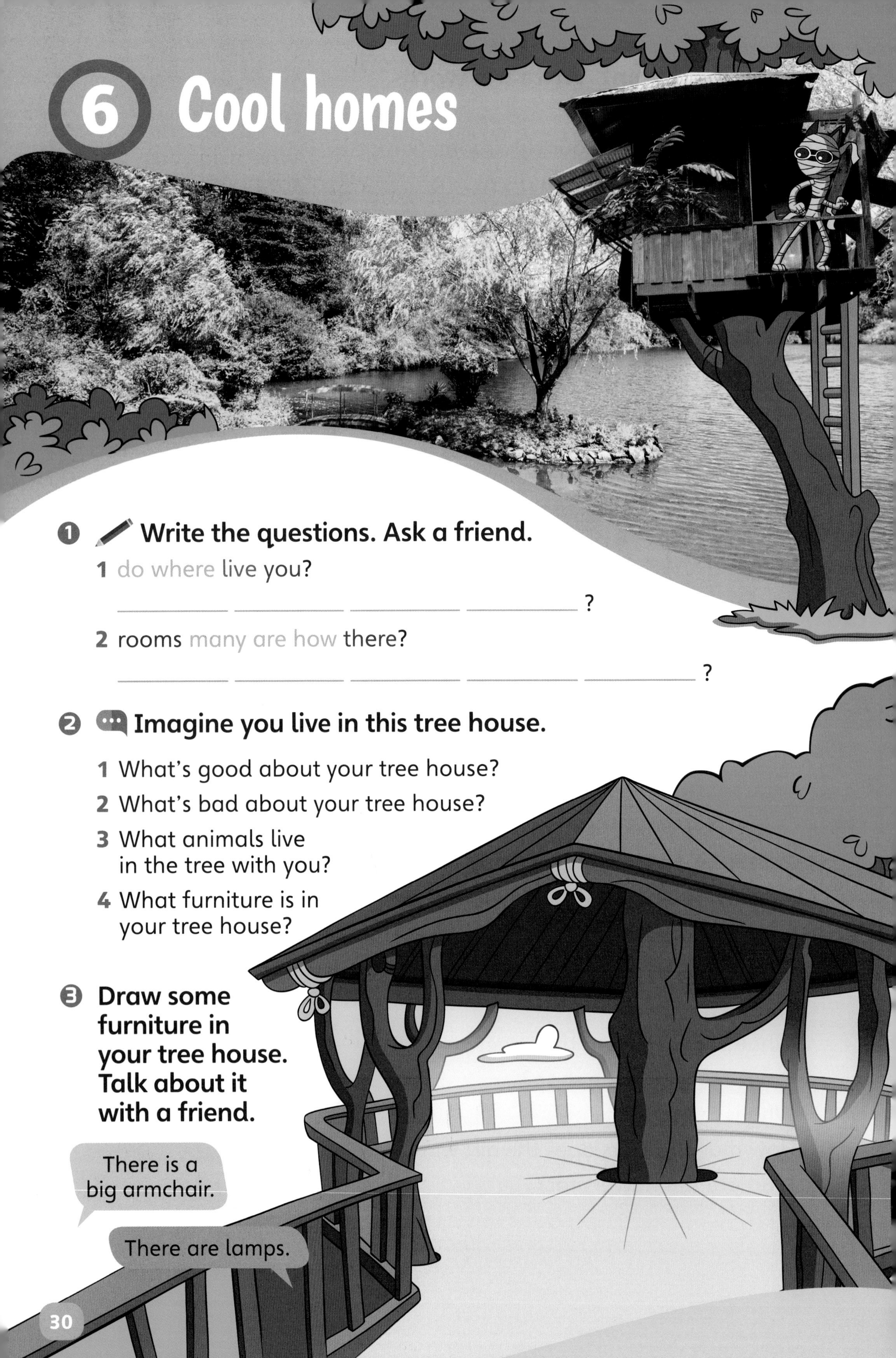

1 Write the questions. Ask a friend.

1 do where live you?

________ ________ ________ ________ ?

2 rooms many are how there?

________ ________ ________ ________ ________ ?

2 Imagine you live in this tree house.

1 What's good about your tree house?

2 What's bad about your tree house?

3 What animals live in the tree with you?

4 What furniture is in your tree house?

3 Draw some furniture in your tree house. Talk about it with a friend.

There is a big armchair.

There are lamps.

4 Can you complete the sentences? Read and write your ideas.

I live in a **1** ____________ near my school.

There is a big kitchen, a dining room, a bathroom and three **2** ____________ .

In my bedroom, there is a white cupboard with my **3** ____________ . I've got a brown box with lots of **4** ____________ . On the wall, there's a mirror and a poster of my favourite animal. It's an **5** ____________ .

My ideas:

1 ____________

2 ____________

3 ____________

4 ____________

5 ____________

5 18 Are your ideas correct? Listen and write the words in task 4.

6 19 Listen and point. Tell a friend what jobs you can see.

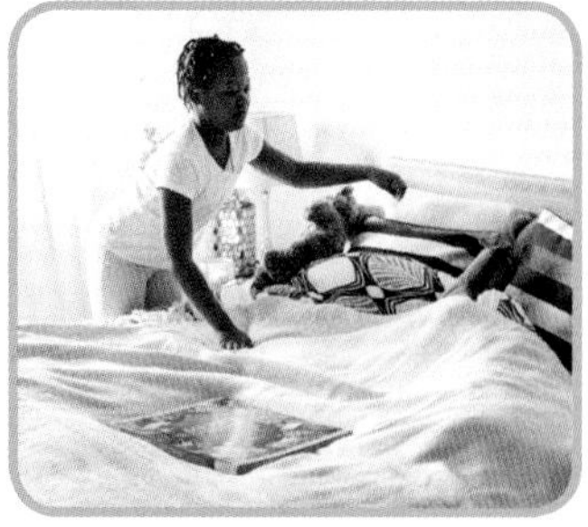

7 20 Listen and match. Who's speaking?

1	Finn	**A**	I make my bed.
2	Cara	**B**	I put my toys in the toy box.
3	Luke	**C**	I put things on the table for dinner.
4	Molly	**D**	I clean the kitchen floor.

THINK BIG
What jobs do you do at home?

1 Talk with a friend.
What can you see?

2 **Read about Molly. Look and write about Finn and Cara.**

Molly's favourite animal is the polar bear. She likes animals.
She loves reading.

1 Finn plays the ______________________
and the ______________ . He loves playing with ______________ .

2 Cara's favourite colours are ______________ and ______________ .
She plays ______________ . She likes ______________ .

3 **Look at page 68. Draw three things in your bedroom. What do we learn about you?**

My favourite ______________ is
______________________ .
I like ______________________ .
I love ______________________ .

TIP! Cover the pictures. Can you guess the missing words?

4 Read this. Choose a word from the box. Write the correct word next to numbers 1–5. There is one example.

Frogs

Do you like frogs? They are fantastic and cool! Frogs have four ___legs___ - two are long and two are short. Many frogs are green but some are grey or yellow. I like to sleep at **1** ________ but they like to sleep in the morning. Some people have a **2** ________ for a pet, but I have a frog! My frog doesn't live in my bathroom or under my **3** ________ . It lives in water in my **4** ________ . And my frog does not close its **5** ________ even when it sleeps! I love my frog!

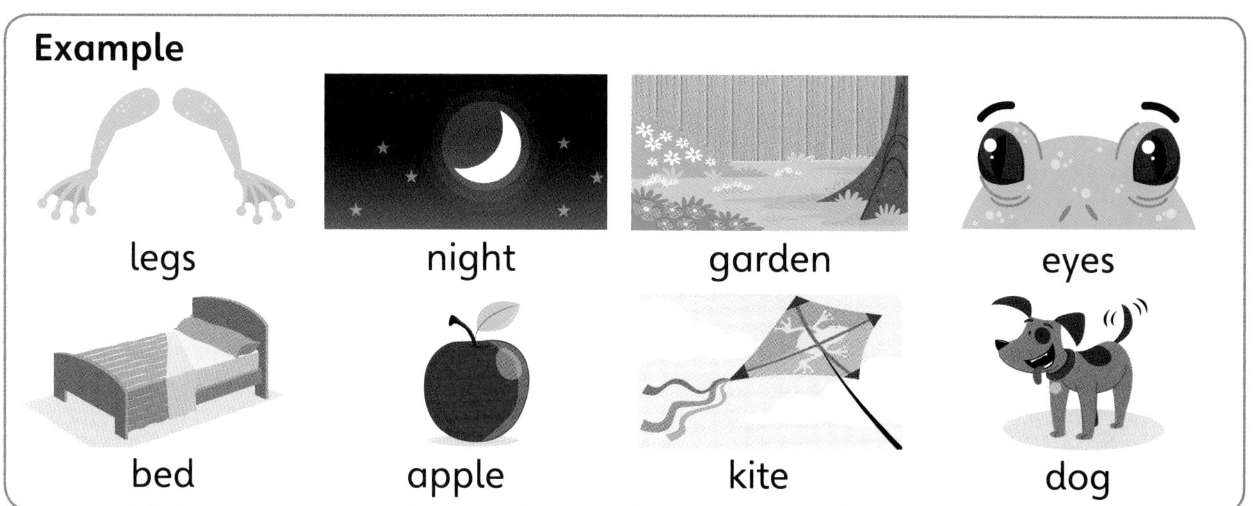

5 Choose words to describe these houses. Which house do / don't you like?

A

B

C

beautiful and scary	funny and silly	fantastic and cool

6 Draw a house. Show your house to your class and talk about it.

This is my house!

It's fantastic and cool!

Review Unit 5

Skills: Reading, Listening and Writing

1 Look at the people in the shops. Read and write the word.

I would like some *flowers*, please.

Can I have that red 1 ______, please?

Here you are. A bag of 2 ______.

Would you like a 3 ______?

Can I have some new 4 ______?

Mark: ___ / 4

2 21 Listen and write the number.

1 

2 

3 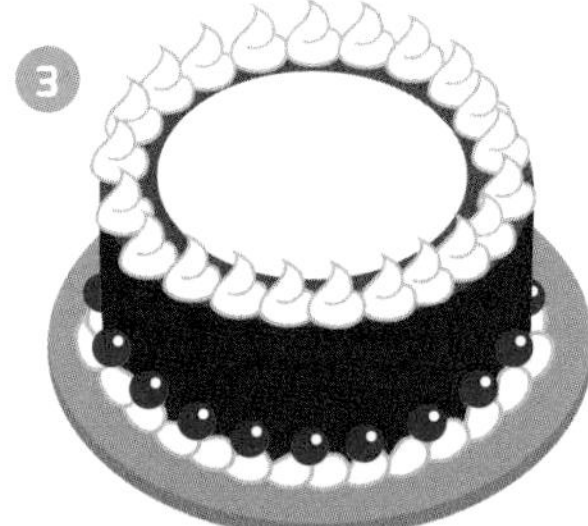

4 

5 

Mark: ___ / 5

3 Read the questions. Choose and write the answers.

1 How old is Pat? ______
2 Who is your teacher? ______
3 How many kiwis would you like? ______
4 How do you spell your name? ______
5 What number is your house? ______

Seven, please.
W-E-B-B.
Mr Brown.
8 years old.
It's 15.

Mark: ___ / 5

Total: ___ / 14

Skills: Reading, Writing and Speaking

1 **Look at the house and number the rooms 1–5.**

Example living room _Room 5_

1 kitchen ______ **3** dining room ______

2 bedroom ______ **4** bathroom ______

Mark: ___ / 4

2 **Look at the house. Where are the people? Read the sentences and write the room.**

Example Tom is sitting on the sofa. He's in the _living room_ .

1 Grace is cleaning the cupboards. She's in the ______ .

2 Alex is putting things on the table for dinner. He's in the ______ .

3 Lucy is making the bed. She's in the ______ .

4 Mark is in the bath. He's in the ______ .

Mark: ___ / 4

3 **Look at the photo. Imagine this is your bedroom. Write the words on the lines.**

My bedroom has got a big w _i_ _n_ _d_ _o_ _w_ . My **1** d _ _ _ is in front of the window. I haven't got a computer. There is a big **2** b _ _ _ _ _ _ _ with lots of books. It's next to my **3** b _ _ . My bedroom is very clean. All my **4** t _ _ _ are in boxes.

Mark: ___ / 4

4 **What's in your bedroom? Say two sentences to a friend.**

Mark: ___ / 4

Total: ___ ___ / 16

7 What would you like?

I can see a pear.

1 What can you see? Tell a friend.

2 Circle the food you can see in task 1.

a coconut	tomatoes	grapes	an orange
a pineapple	a pear	a mango	an onion
a banana	a potato	carrots	peas

3 Draw a person with some of the food from task 2.
Show your picture to a friend.

Look at my picture.

I can see grapes.

4 22 Listen to the chant and say the letters. Then listen and write.

1 l _ _ _ _ _

2 o _ _ _ _ _ _

3 c _ _ _ _ _ _

4 t _ _ _ _ _ _ _

5 Making a cake! Listen and put a tick (✓) or cross (✗). Write the number.

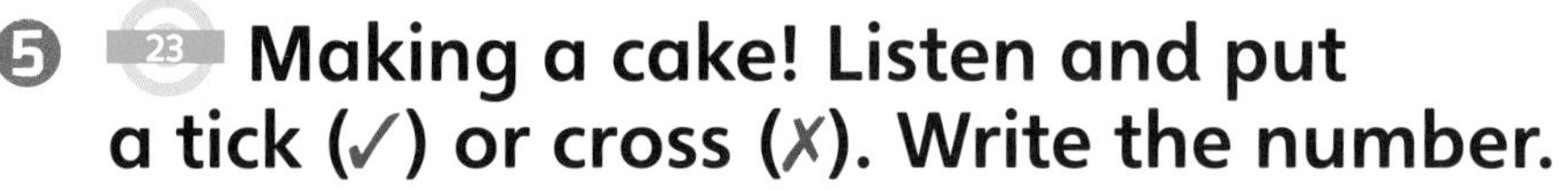

	✓ / ✗	Number
bananas	✓	4
kiwis		
carrots		
eggs		
mango		
lemon		
orange		

6 Read and ask a friend.

This is my favourite fruit. Do you know its name? Can you see a star? It's a star fruit!

This is my favourite fruit. It's a very big fruit. It's a jackfruit. I like eating it with rice and coconut.

1 Do you want to eat a starfruit?

2 Would you like to eat a jackfruit?

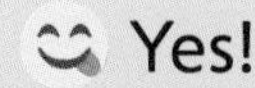

7 Draw a picture and write about your favourite fruit.

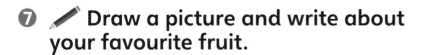

This is my favourite fruit.

It's ______________________________ .

I like eating it with ______________________ .

1 Ask and answer with a friend.

What's this?
It's …
What are these?
They're …

2 Listen and number the pictures.

3 Listen and repeat.

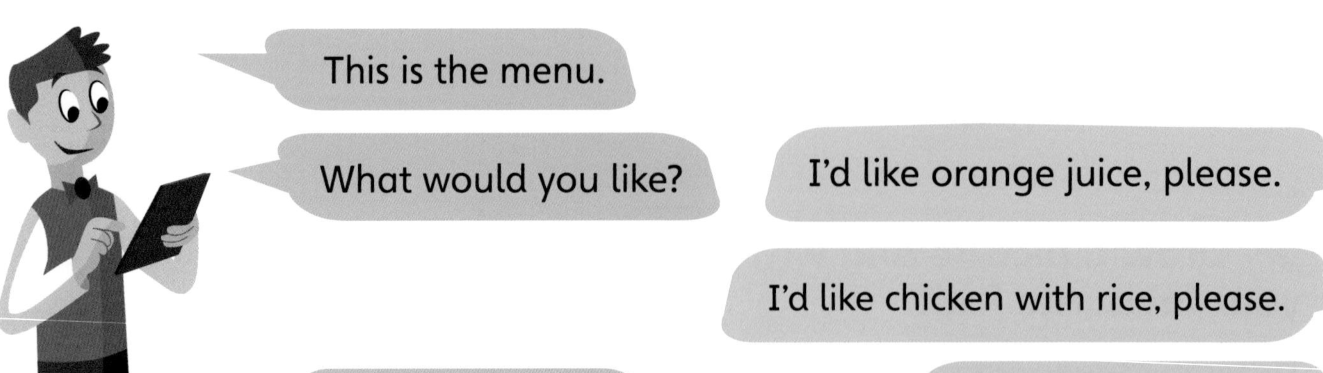

4 Write a menu.

5 Work in groups of three. Imagine you are in a café. Act out.

6 Ask and answer with a friend.

What's your favourite fruit / drink / lunch?

Do you like … ?

8 Let's have fun!

❶ Talk with a friend. What's missing in each picture?

❷ What are the children doing? Choose and write the words in task 1.

dancing   drawing a picture   flying a plane   painting a picture
playing badminton   playing the drums   playing the guitar   singing

❸ 26 Listen to Tom and circle the correct answers.

Example

His favourite class at school is **doing sport** / **painting**.

1 His teacher is **Mrs Green** / **Mrs White**. She's really cool!

2 He likes painting **people** / **animals**.

3 Today, he's **drawing** / **painting** a cat in class.

4 His picture is **not good** / **fantastic**!

4 Write a question. Interview two friends.

Name	____________	____________
What's your favourite sport?	____________	____________
What do you like painting?	____________	____________
Do you like singing?	____________	____________
Do you like ____________ ?	____________	____________

5 Talk to your class about your friends.

Ben likes playing tennis.

6 Talk with a friend. What can you see in the pictures in task 7?

7 27 Listen and tick (✓) the box. There is one example.

What is Sam painting?

A ☐ B ☐ C ✓

1 What is Anna taking to school?

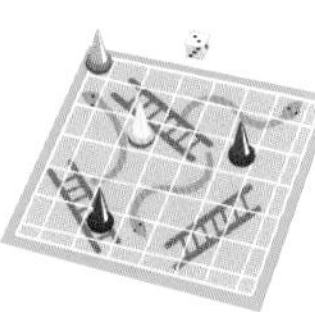

A ☐ B ☐ C ☐

2 What sport is Alice playing?

A ☐ B ☐ C ☐

3 What is Matt taking a photo of?

A ☐ B ☐ C ☐

4 What does Grace play?

A ☐ B ☐ C ☐

5 Which painting is Mark looking at?

A ☐ B ☐ C ☐

1 Look at the painting for one minute. Close your book. How many things can you remember?

There's a bed, a chair …

2 Write these words on the lines.

behind   between   next to   ~~on~~   under

Example There are five pictures ___on___ the wall.

1 There's a chair ________ the table and the bed.

2 There's a table ________ the mirror.

3 There's a picture ________ the window.

4 There are clothes ________ the bed.

THINK BIG

Three of these paintings are by a very famous artist. Can you find out his name?

3 Which paintings do you like? Choose words and write.

scary   funny   silly   beautiful   cool   fantastic

1

It's ________ .

2

It's ________ .

3

It's ________ .

4

It's ________ .

4 Talk to your friends about the paintings in task 3.

I like painting 2.

Me too! It's beautiful!

I don't! I like painting 1.

5 Look at painting 1 again. Read and write *yes* or *no*.

Example The man is playing a guitar. ___yes___

1 There are a lot of people behind the man. ______

2 The women have got fruit in their hair. ______

3 The man is wearing a baseball cap. ______

4 The man is singing. ______

6 Choose and write words about painting 3.

beautiful   boats   ~~cloudy~~   green   painting   sand

It's a ___cloudy___ day. There are four **1** ______ boats on the **2** ______ . There is a red one, a **3** ______ one and two blue ones. Some more **4** ______ are sailing on the sea. I like this **5** ______ .

7 Play a game with a friend.

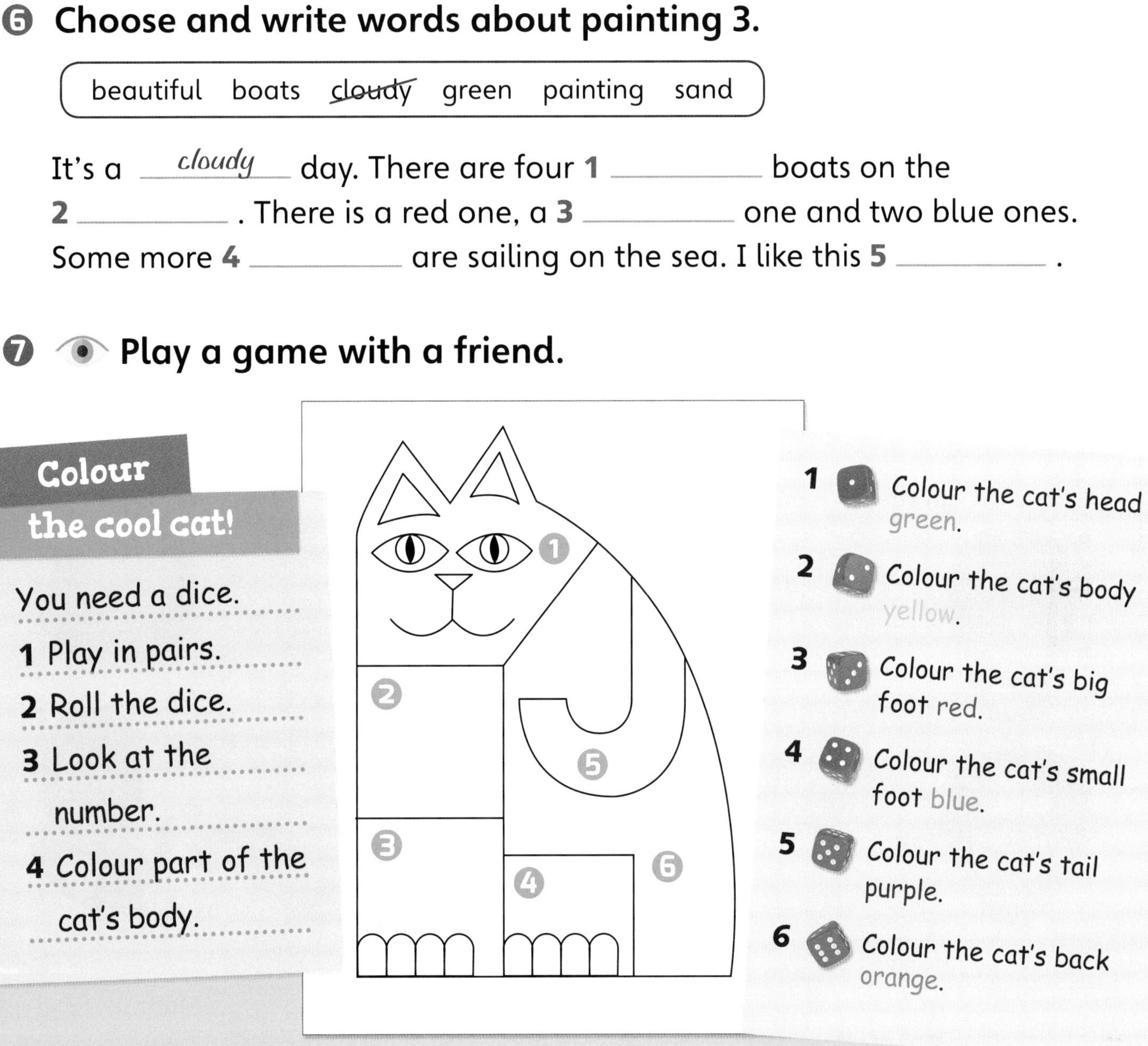

Colour the cool cat!
You need a dice.
1 Play in pairs.
2 Roll the dice.
3 Look at the number.
4 Colour part of the cat's body.
1 Colour the cat's head green.
2 Colour the cat's body yellow.
3 Colour the cat's big foot red.
4 Colour the cat's small foot blue.
5 Colour the cat's tail purple.
6 Colour the cat's back orange.

Review Unit 7

Skills: Listening, Writing and Speaking

1 28 **Whose lunch is it? Listen and match. Write *A*, *B* or *C*.**

Mark: ___ / 3

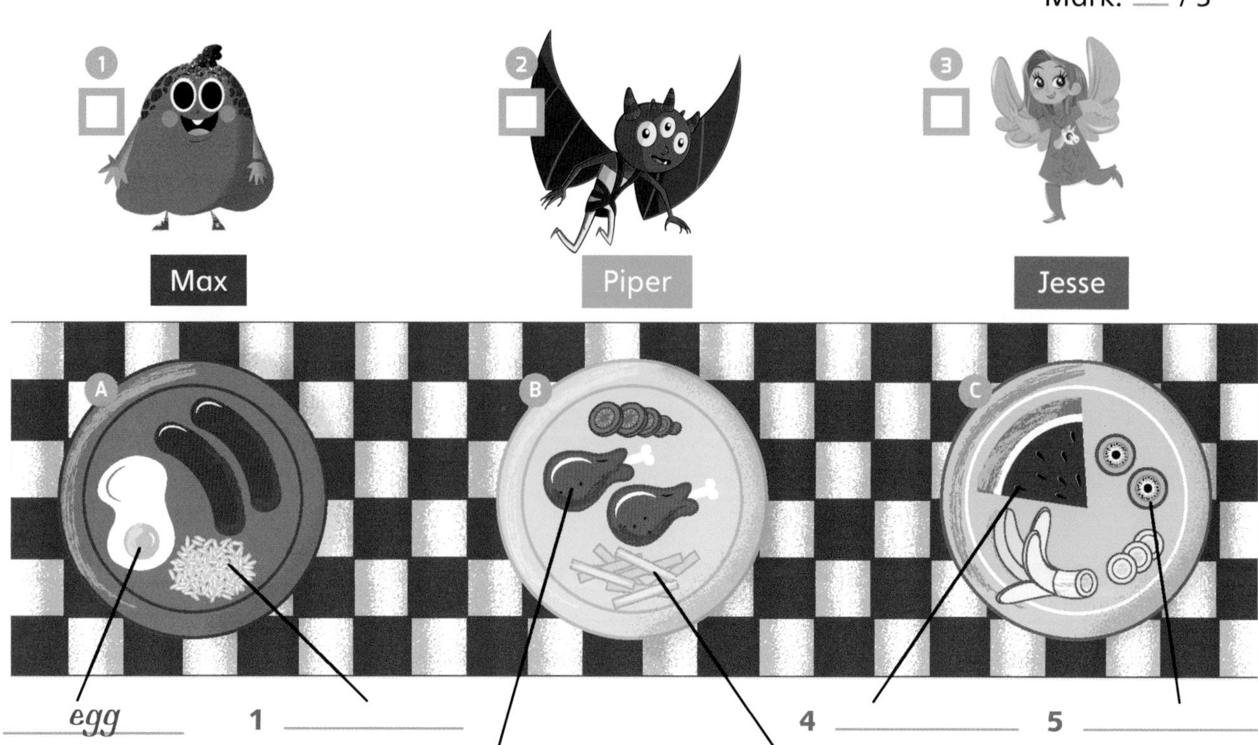

2 **What food can you see? Write on the lines in task 1.**

Mark: ___ / 5

3 **Which food do you like? Ask your partner two questions.**

Do you like …?

What's your favourite …?

Mark: ___ / 4

4 **Read the questions. Number the answers.**

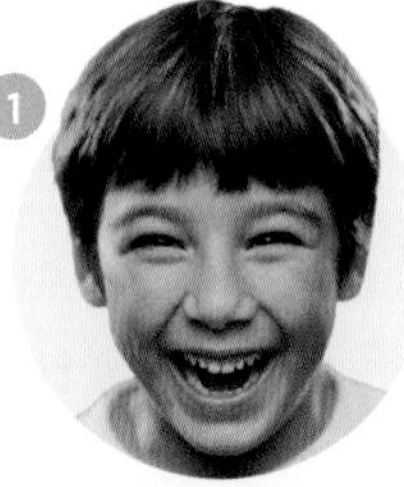

1 Do you like bananas?

2 Would you like a drink?

3 What would you like?

4 Here you are!

Mmm … thank you! ☐

Yes, please. I'd like lemonade. ☐

I'd like a burger, please. ☐

Yes, I do. They're my favourite fruit. 1

Mark: ___ / 3

Total: ___ ___ / 15

Skills: Writing and Reading

1 What does Lucy like doing at school? Write these words.

doing sport taking photos ~~painting~~ playing the piano singing

painting

1 ______

2 ______ 3 ______ 4 ______

Mark: __ / 4

2 Look at Lucy's painting. Write *yes* or *no*.

Example There's a bed under the window. *yes*

1 There are some pictures on the wall. ______

2 There's a bookcase next to the bed. ______

3 There's a cat on the bed. ______

4 There's a door next to the desk. ______

5 There's a rug in front of the bed. ______

Mark: __ / 5

3 Answer the questions about Lucy's painting.

1 How many pictures are there? There are ______ .

2 Do you like the painting? Yes, I ______ . / No, I ______ .

It's ______ .

Mark: __ / 3

Total: __ __ / 12

9 Let's go to the zoo!

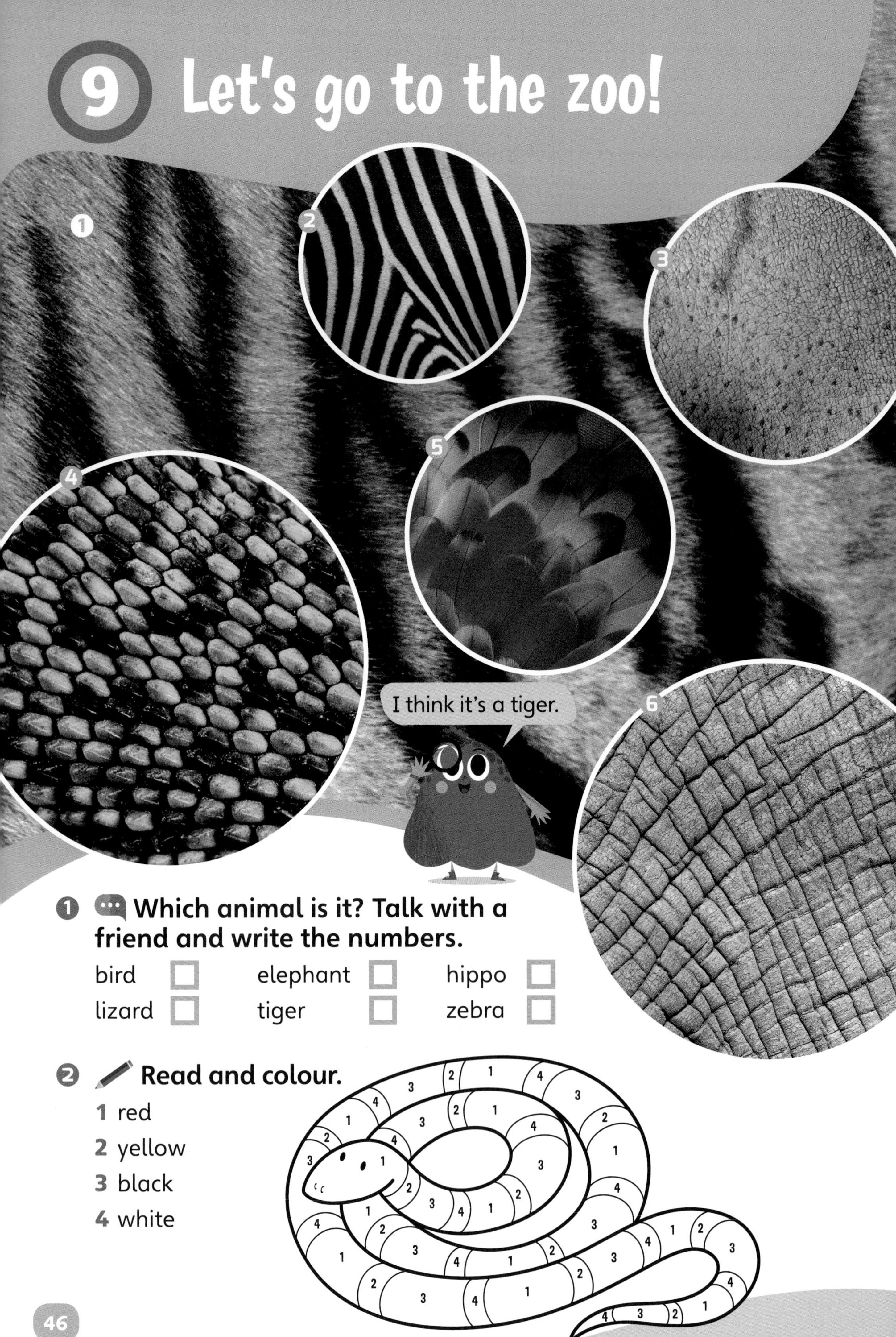

1 Which animal is it? Talk with a friend and write the numbers.

bird	☐	elephant	☐	hippo	☐
lizard	☐	tiger	☐	zebra	☐

2 Read and colour.

1 red
2 yellow
3 black
4 white

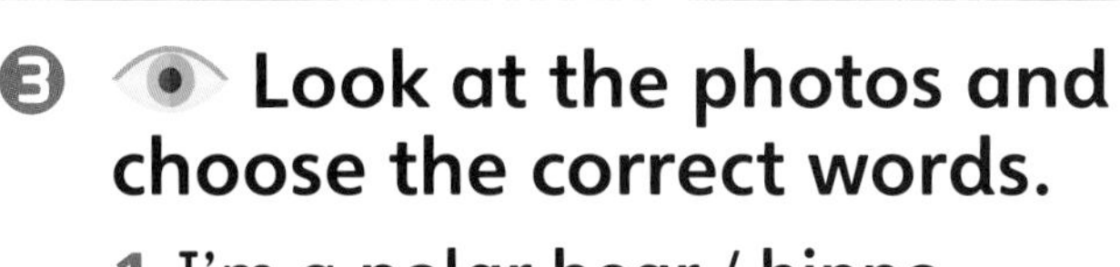

3 Look at the photos and choose the correct words.

1 I'm a **polar bear / hippo**.
2 I'm **white / grey**.
3 I've got **big / small** teeth.
4 I eat **birds / fish**.
5 I live in a **cold / hot** place.
6 I can **fly / swim**.

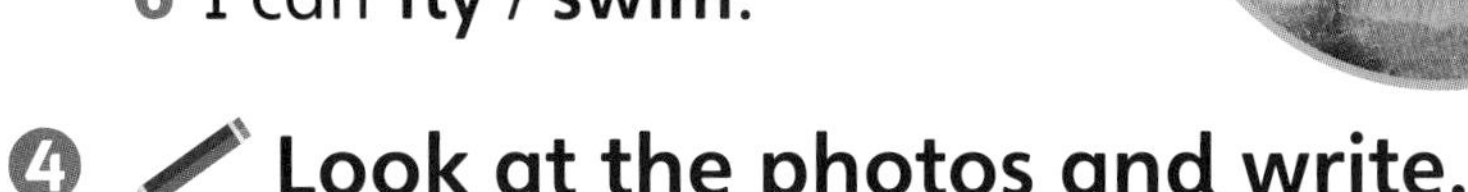

4 Look at the photos and write.

1 I'm a ______________________ .
2 I'm ______________________ .
3 I've got ______________________ .
4 I eat ______________________ .
5 I live ______________________ .
6 I can ______________________ .

THINK BIG
Some crocodiles are 5 metres long!
How long is 5 metres? Find out!

5 Student A: Think of an animal. Student B: Ask three *yes/no* questions.

Does it live in … ?
Does it eat … ?

Has it got … ?

Can it … ?

Is it … ?
Is it a … ?

1 29 **Listen to the song and number the pictures.**

2 **Answer the questions. Draw lines.**

1 Which animal is climbing a tree? — C
2 What is the giraffe doing?
3 Where is the tiger?
4 What is the tiger doing?
5 Which animal is throwing water?

A It's eating leaves.
B It's under the tree.
C the monkey
D the elephant
E It's sleeping.

3 29 **Which of these words are in the song? Tick (✓) the words.**

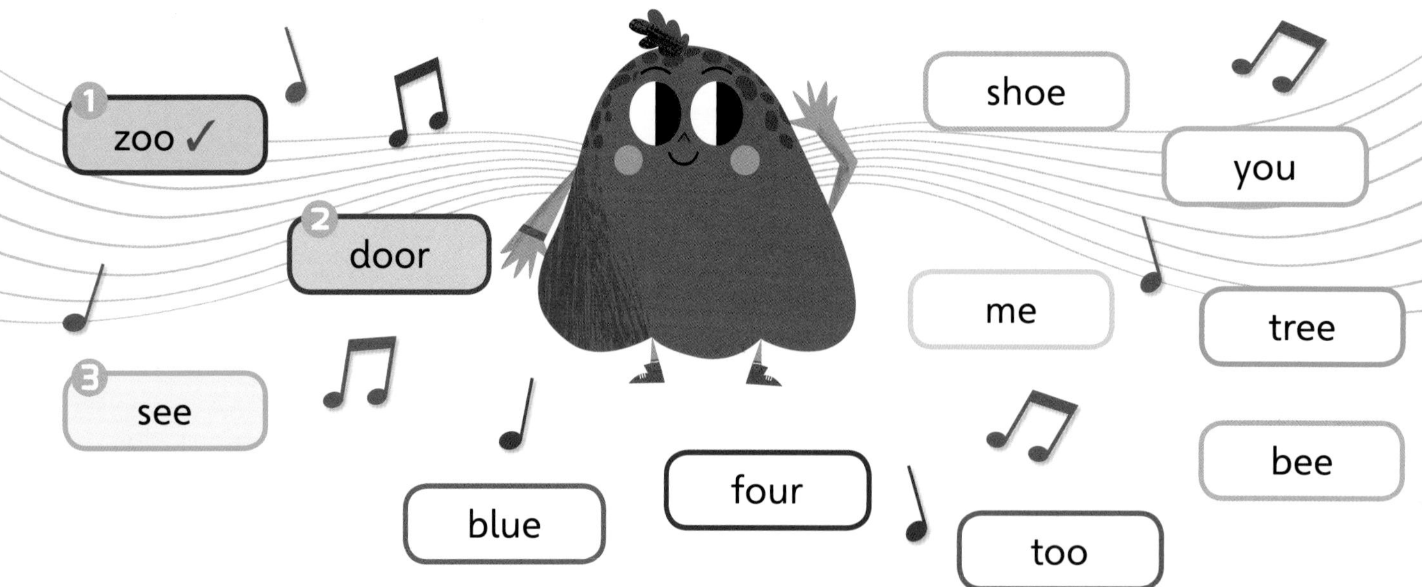

4 30 **How do the eight words sound? Put the words in groups 1–3. Then listen and check.**

❺ Look at the pictures in task 6. What can you see?

❻ Read the questions. Write one-word answers.

Examples

Where are the animals? in the *zoo*

How many animals are there? *five*

1 What is the boy looking at?

a ______________________

2 Where is the balloon?

in the ______________________

3 What is the monkey standing on?

the ______________________

4 Who has got the balloon now?

the ______________________

5 Is the boy sad?

no, he's ______________________

❼ Talk with a friend. Who helps the boy? Who can you help?

I can ______________________ .

TIP!

Write only **one** word in your answers.

10 Fun on the beach

1 (31) Close your eyes and listen to four sounds. Then open your eyes and tick (✓).

2 Look at the photos in task 1 and write the words.

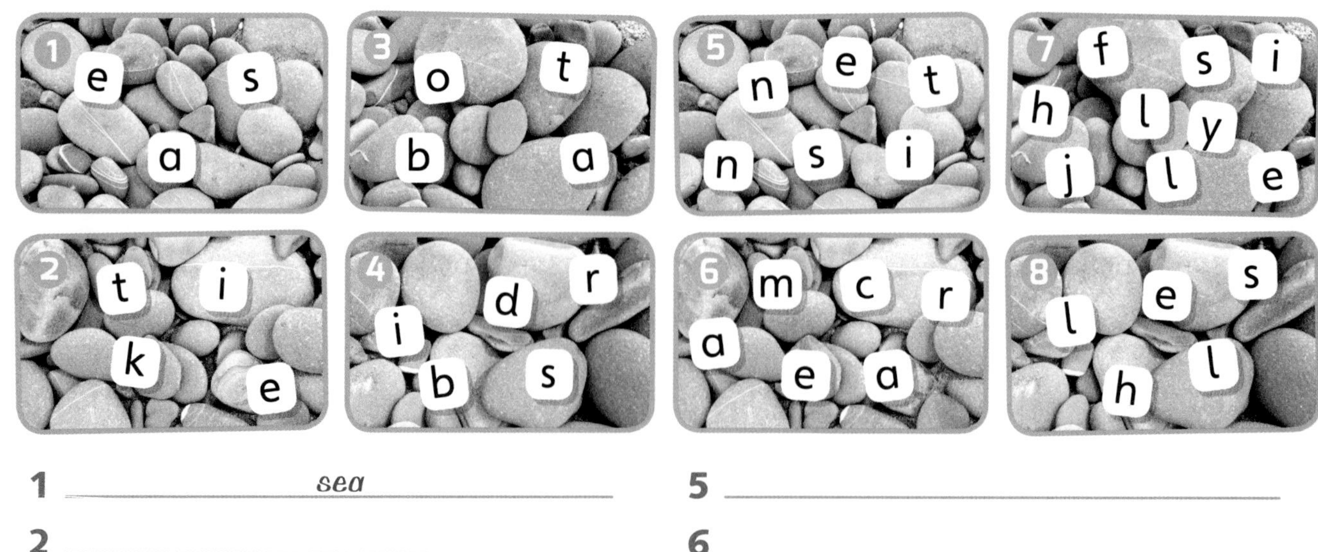

1 *sea*

2 ______

3 ______

4 ______

5 ______

6 ______

7 ______

8 ______

3 Look at the photos in task 1. Answer with a friend.

1 Which things do you play with on the beach?
2 Which things can you see on the beach?
3 Which things do you find in the sea?

4 Talk with a friend. What do you like doing at the beach?

I like running on the beach.
So do I!

I like playing tennis.
I don't!

5 32 Listen and colour. There is one example.

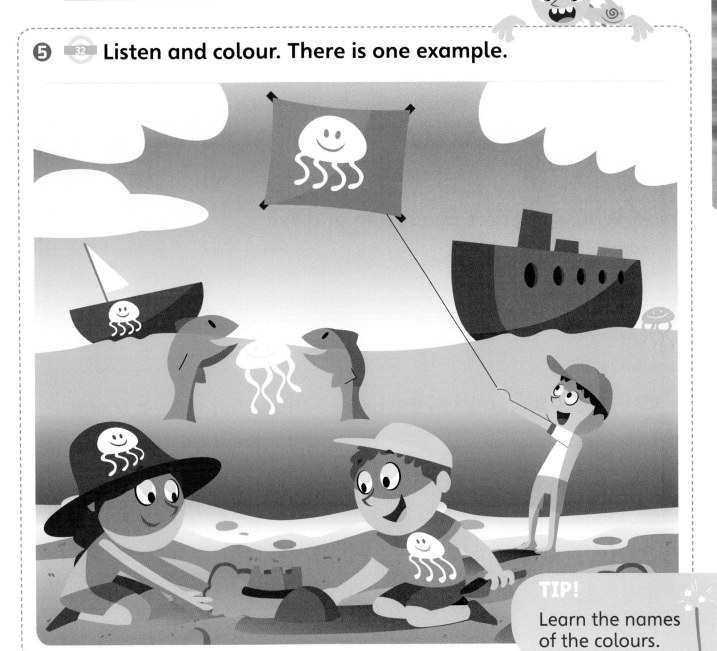

TIP!
Learn the names of the colours.

1 Look at the pictures and tick (✓) the things on each list.

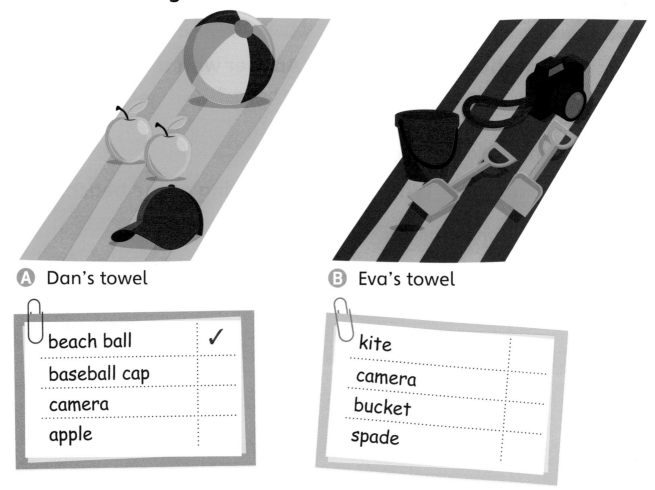

A Dan's towel

beach ball	✓
baseball cap	
camera	
apple	

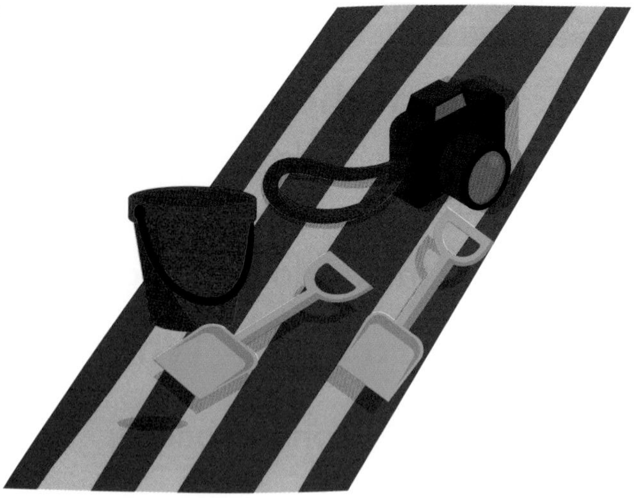

B Eva's towel

kite	
camera	
bucket	
spade	

2 Write sentences about Dan and Eva.

Example Dan's got a *beach ball*.

1 Dan's got two ________________.

2 Dan hasn't got a ________________.

3 Eva's got ________________.

4 Eva ________________.

3 What do you take to the beach? Draw and show a friend.

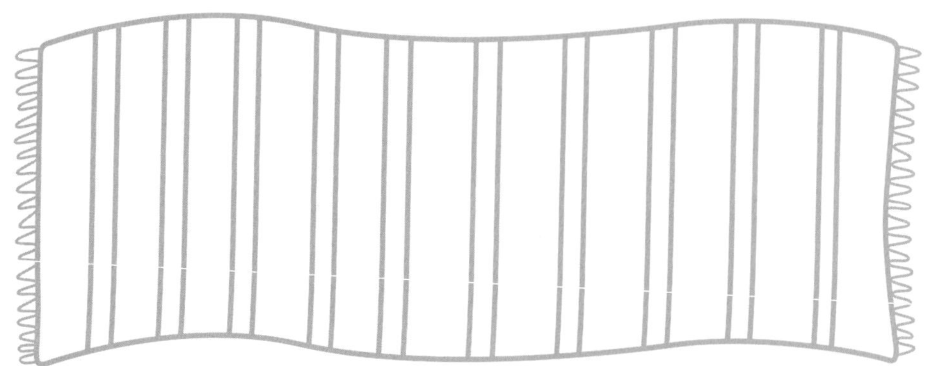

I've got …

4 [33] What does Dan like doing? Listen and tick (✓).

5 [33] Listen again. Circle *yes* or *no*.

Example Dan likes flying a kite. yes / (no)

1 He plays tennis with his sister. yes / no

2 He's got a camera. yes / no

3 He doesn't like making sandcastles. yes / no

6 Make a sandcastle with Sam! Choose and write the words.

put ~~draw~~ make find take

Draw a circle in the sand.

3 ________ shells on the beach.

1 ________ sand in the bucket with a spade.

4 ________ a photo of your fantastic sandcastle!

2 ________ a big sandcastle!

Sam sees shells on the sandcastle!

7 [34] What does Piper say? Listen and repeat.

Review Unit 9 

Skills: Reading, Listening and Writing

1 **Look at the picture. Read and write *yes* or *no*.**

Example A monkey is eating a banana in the tree. ___*yes*___

1 Two hippos are swimming in the water. ______
2 A zebra is running behind the tiger. ______
3 An elephant is standing in the water. ______
4 A giraffe is sitting next to the elephant. ______
5 A bear is catching a fish from the water. ______

Mark: ___ / 5

2 35 **Which animal is it? Listen and number the animals in the picture.**

Mark: ___ / 6

3 **What are the animals doing in the picture? Write five sentences in your notebook.**

Example *The elephant is throwing water.*

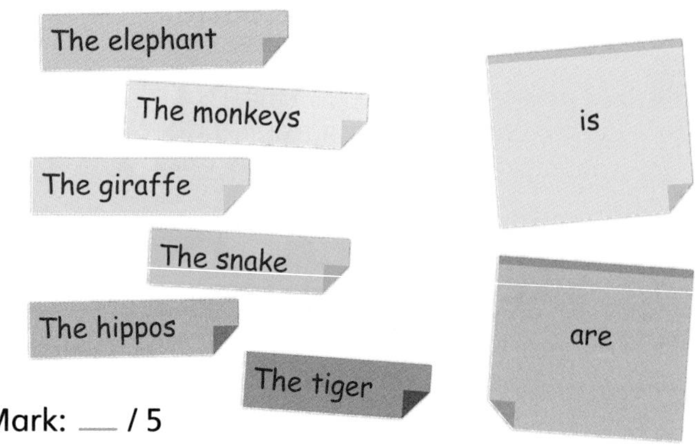

eating the tree.
swimming in the water.
playing in the tree.
running.
throwing water.
sleeping under the tree.

Mark: ___ / 5
Total: ___ ___ / 16

Review Unit 10

Skills: Speaking, Writing and Reading

1 Look at the beach and talk with a friend. What are the children doing?

Look! A girl is swimming.

Mark: ___ / 6

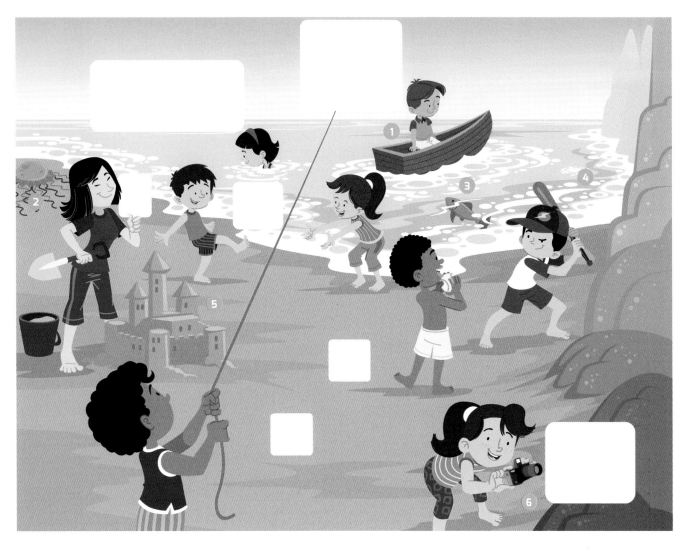

2 Write the names of the things in the picture.

1 b _o_ _a_ _t_
2 j ___ ___ ___ ___ ___ ___ ___ ___
3 f ___ ___ ___
4 s ___ ___
5 s ___ ___ ___ ___ ___ ___ ___ ___ ___
6 c ___ ___ ___ ___ ___

Mark: ___ / 5

3 Read and draw the missing things in the picture.

1 A boy is flying a kite.
2 A girl is taking a photo of a bird.
3 A woman is eating an ice cream.
4 Two children are playing with a ball.
5 There are two shells on the sand.
6 There is a ship on the sea.

Mark: ___ / 6

Total: ___ ___ / 17

11 Our things

Jade Tom Sara

1 **Look at the picture. Answer the questions.**

1 How many children can you see?

2 What are the children doing?

2 36 **Listen to the song. Is the picture in task 1 correct?**

3 **Whose are the things? Look, read and choose.**

Examples It's **Sara's** / **Jade's** watch.

It's a phone. It's **hers** / **his**.

1  They're **Tom's** / **Jade's** glasses.

2  It's a bag. It's **hers** / **his**.

3  It's **Sara's** / **Jade's** baseball cap.

4  It's a jacket. It's **hers** / **his**.

4 37 **Listen and circle the words with the /ɪz/ sound.**

watches cameras sunglasses horses baseball caps sandwiches

5 [38] What can you see in the photos? Listen and number.

What a cool school trip!

6 Match the sentences to the photos. Write A–F.

1 We're walking in the forest. ___
2 We're listening to our teacher. A
3 She's eating her lunch. ___
4 We're giving food to the goats. ___
5 We're standing next to the school bus. ___
6 He's looking at the flowers. ___

7 Talk with a friend. Where do you like going on school trips?

I like this.

So do I. It's fun!

I don't! It's scary!

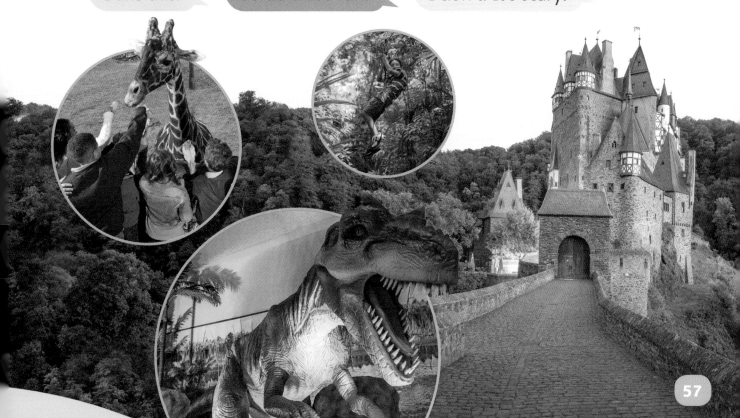

1 What's missing? Read and draw in the desks.

1 Hi I'm Diego! This is my desk. There are two **rulers**, some **pencils** and my favourite blue **baseball cap**. I've got a **painting** of this lovely butterfly!

2 Hello everyone! I'm Joel. There are lots of things in my desk. I have three **books**, a red **baseball cap**, **a tablet** and a **ball**.

3 Hello, I'm Hana. This is my desk. It's my favourite colour – red. I have a **book** to read, a yellow **baseball cap**, my **glasses** and this beautiful paper **ball**!

2 Point to the things in the desks. Ask and answer.

Whose is this?

It's Diego's.

3 Whose is this? Write *mine* or *yours*.

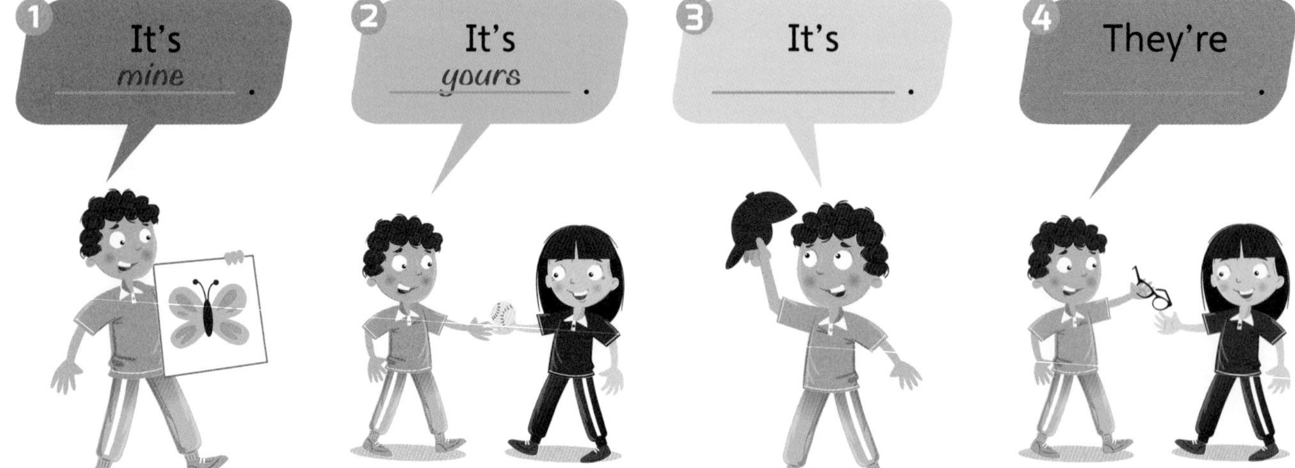

1 It's mine.
2 It's yours.
3 It's ______.
4 They're ______.

4 Draw four of your things. Ask and answer with a friend.

What's this?
Whose is this?
What colour is it?

5 Work in groups. Read the instructions and play a game!

1 Sit in a circle. Put your pictures on the floor.

2 Choose a picture.

3 Ask and answer.

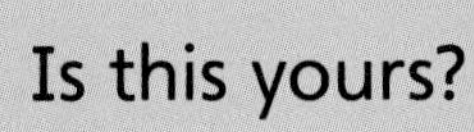

Is this yours?

Yes, it is!

12 What's your favourite game?

1 Look and write the words.

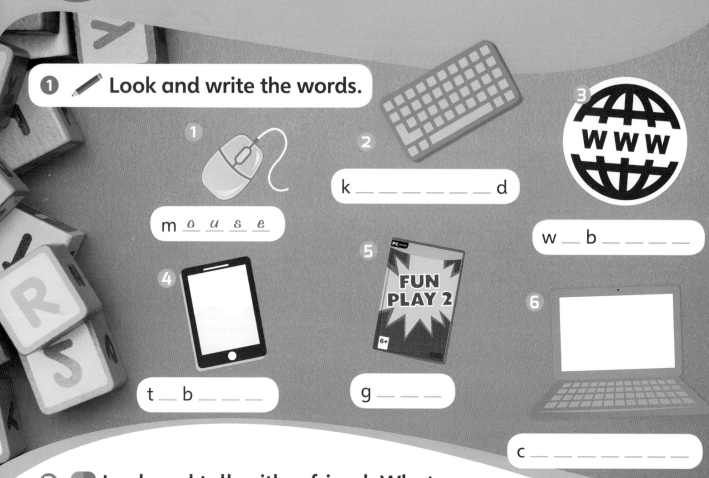

1 m o u s e

2 k _ _ _ _ _ _ d

3 w _ b _ _ _ _

4 t _ b _ _ _

5 g _ _ _

FUN PLAY 2

6 c _ _ _ _ _ _ _

2 Look and talk with a friend. What are the children doing? Do you like these games?

He's singing.

I like this one!

This is my favourite!

3 39 Listen and number the pictures in task 2.

4 Look and read. Write *yes* or *no*.

Examples

The girl is holding her tablet. ___no___

There are four people in the room. ___yes___

Questions

1 There is an armchair next to the door. ______
2 The man has got the mouse in his hand. ______
3 The boy is singing. ______
4 The woman is looking at her tablet. ______
5 The dog is behind the sofa. ______

5 40 Listen and clap. Then say the chant.

Websites are fun!
Tablets are cool!
Computers are fantastic,
But playing tennis rules!

6 Write your own chant.

______ FUN!
______ COOL!
______ FANTASTIC,
But ______!

1 Look at the photos and talk with a friend. What are the children doing?

1 

2 

3 

4 

THINK BIG

Which pictures show good ideas?

2 41 Listen and check your ideas. Which of these things do you do?

3 Choose words and write.

choose ~~open~~ play
read write

1 

___Open___ the app.

2 

________ your name.

3 

________ about the game.

4 

________ a character.

5 

________ the game!

4 Look at the picture and answer the questions.

Example What's the character's name?

1 What colour are his clothes?
2 What can he do?
3 Where does he live?
4 Where is he going?

His name is *Captain Zoom*. His clothes are green and
1 ____________. He can 2 ____________. He lives in a big
3 ____________. He's going to the 4 ____________ in the sea.

ZOOM
ZOOM
Do you want to play my game! It's fun!

5 Make a computer game character! Think about the questions and make notes. Then look at page 69.

1 What is your character's name? ____________
2 What does it wear? ____________
3 What can it do? ____________
4 Where does it live? ____________

6 Show your game to a friend and talk about it.

What a cool character!
This is my character!

Review Unit 11

Skills: Listening, Writing and Reading

1 42 **What do Ann and Matt like doing? Listen and tick (✓) the photos.**

1 
2 
3 
4 

Mark: ___ / 4

2 42 **Listen again and circle Ann's things in red and Matt's things in green.**

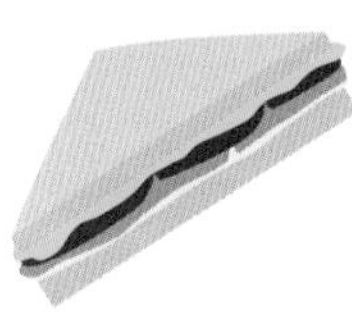

Mark: ___ / 5

3 Answer the question.

Whose is the blue baseball cap?
It's *Matt's* / It's *his* .

Whose is the red baseball cap?
It's ________ / It's ________ .

Mark: ___ / 2

4 Match the questions and answers.

1 Do you like my photos?
2 Is this your camera?
3 Where do the children live?
4 How many children are there?
5 Are these your books?
6 What are you doing?

A In the country.
B Yes, they're cool!
C Ssshh! I'm listening to the teacher!
D No. They're Tom's.
E Yes, it is. It's mine.
F There are two.

Mark: ___ / 5
Total: ___ ___ / 16

Skills: Reading and Writing

1 Choose the words and write.

tablet keyboard mouse ~~website~~ phone

1 I **look at** the *website*.

2 I **read** on my ______.

3 I **write** on the ______.

4 I **choose** with the ______.

5 I **listen** to music on my ______.

Mark: __ / 4

2 Look at the game and choose the answers.

Example What's the character's name?

It's *Captain Zoom* / *Jesse.*

1 What colour are her clothes?

They're **beautiful** / **blue and pink**.

2 Where is she?

She's **under the sea** / **on the beach**.

3 What can she do?

She can **run** / **swim**.

4 Where is she going?

She's going to **the shell** / **boat**.

Mark: __ / 4

3 Answer the questions.

1 What's your name? ______

2 What are you wearing? ______

3 Where do you live? ______

4 What's your favourite game? ______

Mark: __ / 8

Total: __ __ / 16

Pairwork

Unit 2 page 13

7 Make a word tree!

1 Find leaves in the park.

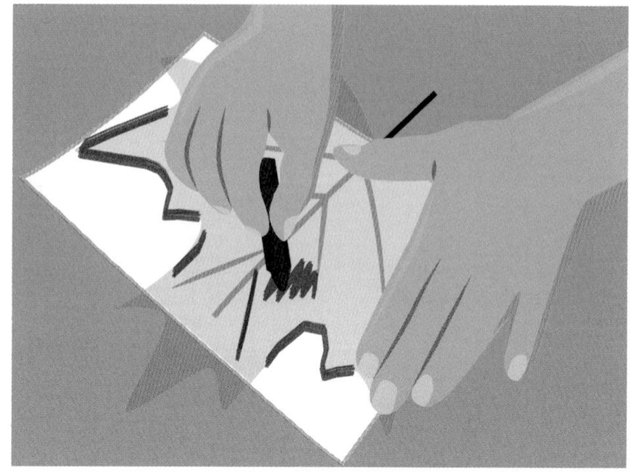

2 Put the leaves under paper and rub with a crayon.

3 Cut out the leaves.

4 Write your favourite park words on your leaves.

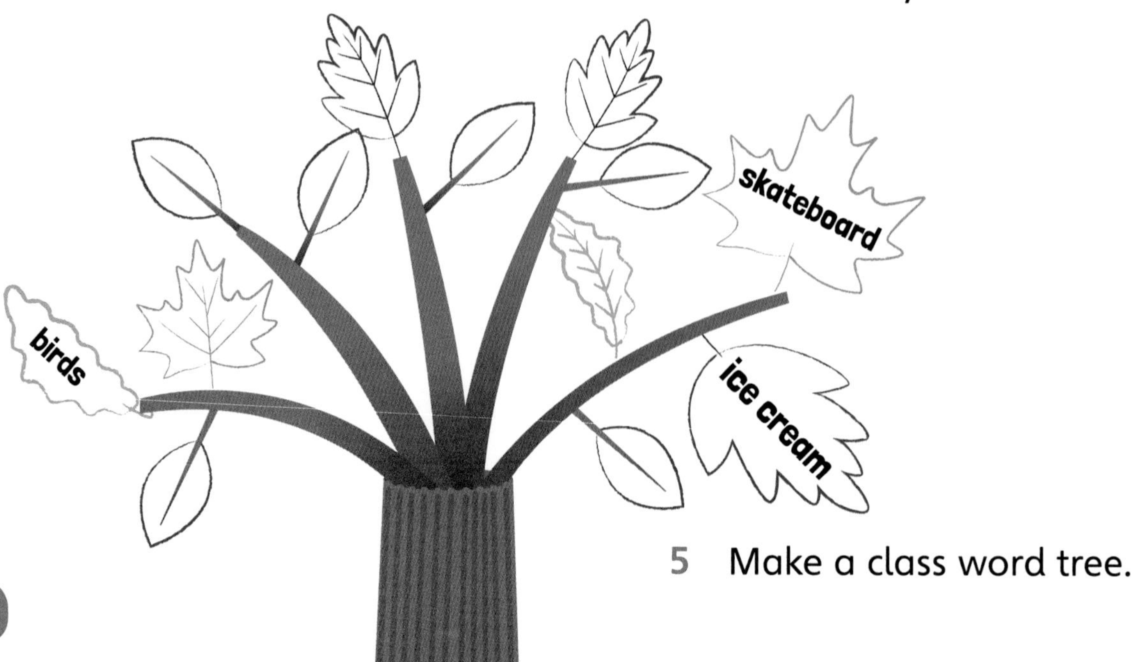

5 Make a class word tree.

Unit 3 page 19

❼ Make a pop-up birthday card!

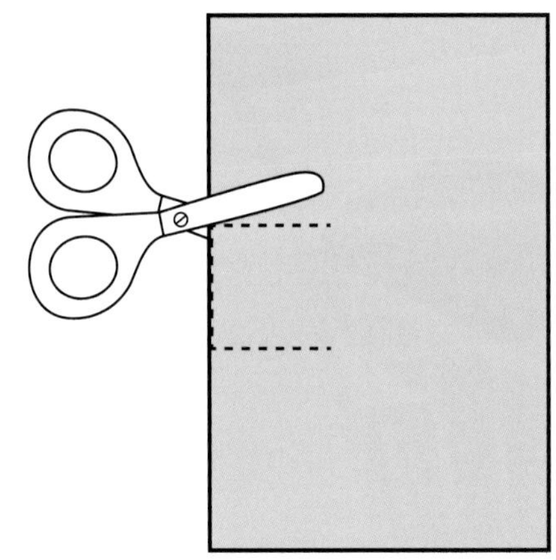

1 Fold and cut your card.

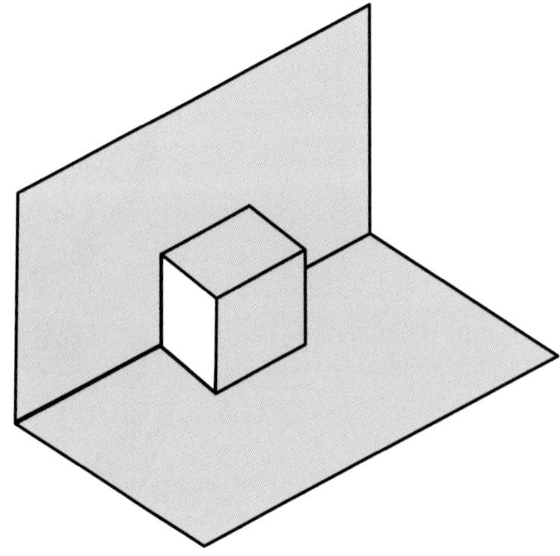

2 Open the card to make the box.

3 Draw your birthday picture.

4 Stick your picture on the box.

5 Write your card.

6 Give your card to a friend.

Pairwork

Unit 5 page 26

❷ **Look at the trolley. How many things can you remember in 30 seconds?**

Unit 6 page 32

❸ **Draw three things in your bedroom.**

What can you see in my bedroom?

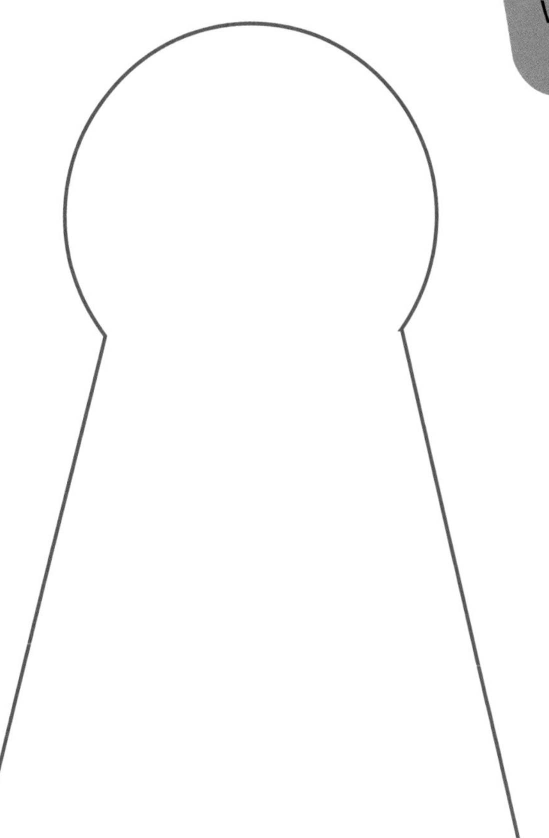

Unit 12 page 63

5 Make a computer game character! Draw and write.

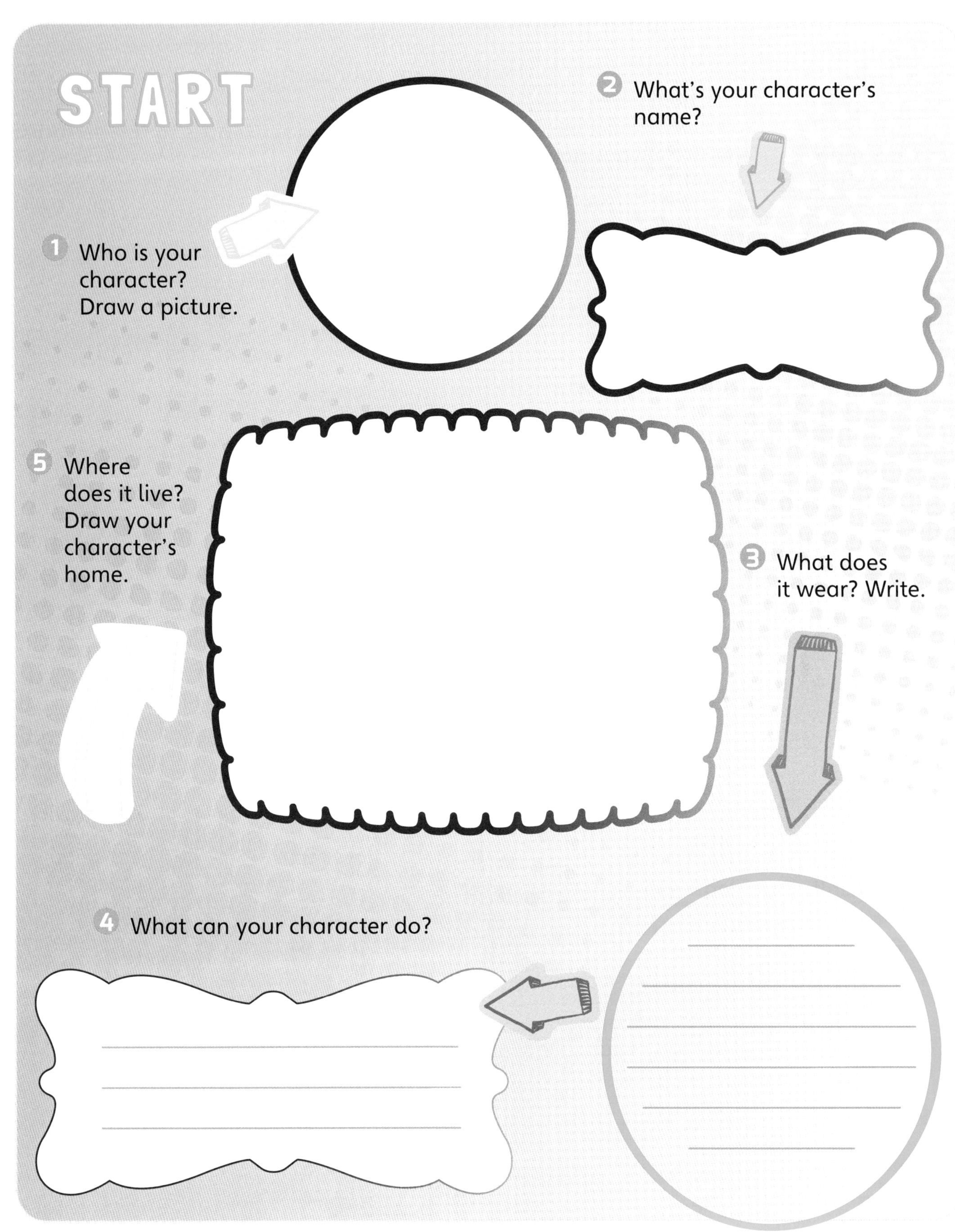

START
1 Who is your character? Draw a picture.
2 What's your character's name?
3 What does it wear? Write.
4 What can your character do?
5 Where does it live? Draw your character's home.

Unit 1

Question words *what*, *how*, *who*, *how many*

What colour is your bag? **What's** in your bag? **What** do you do at school? **How** do you go to school? **How many** students are in your class? **Who's** your best friend?

what's = what is
who's = who is

1 Write the question words.

1 A: ________ have you got on your desk?
B: A book, a pencil and a ruler.

2 A: ________ is that boy?
B: It's Hugo.

3 A: ________ chocolates are there?
B: Ten!

4 A: ________ do you learn English?
B: I go to classes and read books.

Have got for possession

What **have** you **got** in your bag?	
Have you **got** a pen?	Yes, I **have**. / No, I **haven't**.
She **has got** / She'**s got** a cat. She **hasn't got** a dog.	

2 Complete the sentences. Use *have got*.

1 What ________ you ________ in your bedroom?

2 Ben ________ a teddy bear called Fred.

3 Q: ________ you ________ a helicopter?
A: Yes, I ________ .

4 Q: ________ she ________ a pet?
A: No, she ________ .

Unit 2

Imperatives

Walk on the grass. **Eat** your lunch.	**Don't walk** on the grass. **Don't eat** your lunch.

1 Match the sentences to the pictures.

1 Enjoy your food! ________
2 Be quiet! ________
3 Sleep well. ________
4 Close the window. ________

A

B

C

D
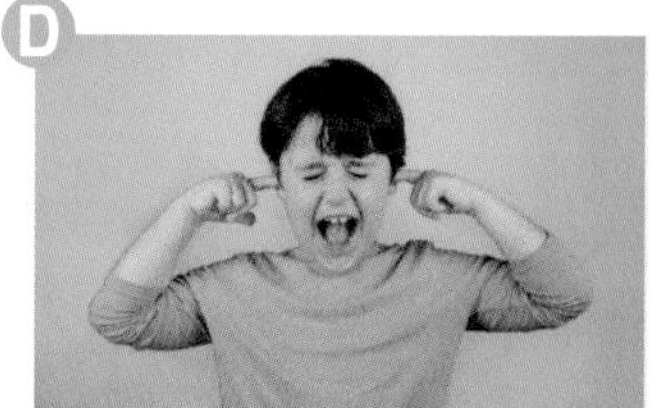

2 Complete the sentences with a verb from the box.

drink smile go show draw ~~bounce~~

Example *Don't bounce* the ball. (✗)

1 I'm tired. ____________ to sleep! (✓)

2 ____________ in my book. (✗)

3 Let's take a photo. ____________ ! (✓)

4 ____________ that juice. It's mine. (✗)

5 ____________ me your drawing. (✓)

Unit 3

Question word *where*

Where are the presents? **Where** do you meet your friends?

1 Match the questions to the answers.

1 Where does Tom sit?
2 Where do they live?
3 Where does Mark sleep?
4 Where is Sue?

A In a big bed.
B In the playground.
C In an apartment.
D At the front of the classroom.

Prepositions of place (*on*, *under*, *next to*, *in front of*, *behind*, *between*)

There's a teddy bear **on** the chair. The mouse is **under** the sofa. The sweets are **next to** the chocolates. The bike is **in front of** the house. The ball is **behind** the dog. The monster is **between** the table and the balloons.

2 Write the prepositions.

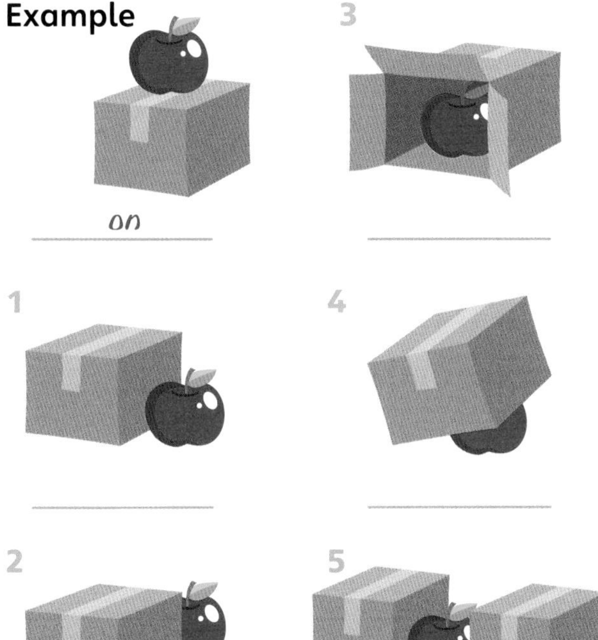

Unit 4

What (*a*/*an*/–) + adjective + noun

What **a** cool alien! What **an** angry robot! What fantastic shoes!

1 Complete the sentences with *What a/an/–* and the adjective.

1 ____________ pineapple! (nice)
2 ____________ hats! (beautiful)
3 ____________ hippo! (old)
4 ____________ room! (clean)
5 ____________ feet! (big)
6 ____________ monster! (ugly)
7 ____________ film! (scary)
8 ____________ clothes! (cool)

Unit 5

Determiners *a*, *the*, *some*

I've got **a** book. I've got **an** apple. I've got **some** books and **some** apples. What's the name of the street?

1 Choose the correct answers.

1 I've got **a** / **an** pet.
2 She's got **a** / **an** elephant.
3 They've got **a** / **an** question.
4 We've got **a** / **an** motorbike.
5 He's got **a** / **an** orange.
6 You've got **a** / **an** computer.

2 Complete the sentences with *a*, *an*, *the* or *some*.

1 Have you got ________ pen?
2 ________ ball under the chair is red.
3 There are ________ monkeys in the tree.
4 I want ________ apple.
5 I want ________ grapes.
6 ________ bus at school is green.

Unit 6

Present simple questions with *do* and short answers (*Yes, I do* / *No, I don't*)

Do you **like** frogs?	Yes, I **do**. / No, I **don't**.
Does she/he/the monster **make** her/his/its bed?	Yes, she/he/it **does**. / No, she/he/it **doesn't**.
Do they **clean** the floor?	Yes, they **do**. / No, they **don't**.

1 Put the questions in the correct order.

1 you / do / badminton? / play
____
2 like / she / music? / does
____
3 clean / does / he / bedroom? / his
____
4 photos? / do / take / you
____

2 Write questions.

Example (the robot / sing songs)
Does the robot sing songs?

1 (Abdullah / like pizza)
____
2 (Lucy and Kim / read many books)
____
3 (you / know the answer)
____

3 Answer the questions.

1 Do you walk to school?
________ (✓)
2 Does the monster eat bananas?
________ (✗)
3 Do Sofia and Matt like cheese?
________ (✗)

Grammar fun!

Unit 7

Would like + noun or verb

I'd like a drink. She**'d like to eat** a starfruit.	
Would you **like to eat** a jackfruit?	Yes, I **would**. / No, I **wouldn't**.

I'd = I would
She'd = She would

1 Complete the sentences with *would like* and the noun or verb.

1 Anna ________________ . (an apple)
2 Nick ________________ . (eat chilli)
3 Matteo ________________ . (some new trousers)
4 Eva and Sam ________ . (swim in the sea)
5 ________ you ________ ? (come to my house)
6 ________ Ben ________ ? (a sandwich)

2 Answer the questions.

1 Would you like a drink?
________________________ (✗)
2 Would you like to take a picture?
________________________ (✓)
3 Would Lucy like to play?
________________________ (✓)

Unit 8

Adverbs: *really*, *very*

This painting is **very** famous.
She's **really** cool!

1 Put the sentences in the correct order.

1 doll / beautiful. / is / really / that
____
2 dirty. / is / bike / my / very
____
3 really / this / burger / good. / is
____
4 hair / long. / is / very / my
____
5 spiders / cool. / really / are
____

2 Add *very* or *really* to the sentences.

1 This watermelon is nice.
____
2 My skateboard is old.
____
3 That monkey is silly.
____
4 The jellyfish is scary.
____
5 My bedroom is clean.
____

Unit 9

Can for ability

Can you see? I **can** understand English. I **can't** see without my glasses.

1 Match the sentences to the pictures.

1 The baby can wave. ☐
2 She can't sing. ☐
3 He can play the guitar. ☐
4 He can't carry the suitcase. ☐
5 They can read Chinese. ☐

A

B

C
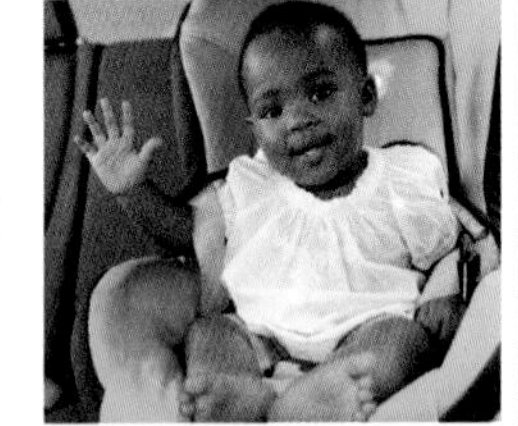

D

E

Unit 10

Nouns: countable and uncountable

Countable Dan's got a beach ball. Eva's got two spades.
Uncountable Would you like **some water** / **rice** / **milk**? Would you like to listen to **some music**?
Irregular There are three **fish** in the sea! There are two **people** / **men** / **women** / **mice** / **children**. Cats have four **feet**.

1 Look and write. Use a number for countable nouns and *some* for uncountable nouns.

1 *some rice*
2 *two apples*
3 __________
4 __________
5 __________

Can for requests/permission

Can I **colour** the jellyfish? **Can** I **have** some birthday cake?

2 Put the sentences in the correct order.

1 throw / ball? / the / I / can

____

2 some / have / water? / can / I

____

3 question? / ask / I / can / a

____

Grammar fun!

Unit 11

Possessive pronouns *mine*, *yours*, *his*, *hers*, *ours*, *theirs*

Whose watch is it?	It's my watch. = It's **mine**. It's your watch. = It's **yours**. It's his watch. = It's **his**. It's her watch. = It's **hers**. It's our watch. = It's **ours**. It's their watch. = It's **theirs**.

1 Complete the sentences with the correct possessive pronoun.

1 Is that robot __________ ? (you)
2 This is __________ ! (me)
3 That's not my classroom, it's __________ . (they)
4 I like my hat but I love __________ . (she)
5 This puppy is __________ . (we)
6 Those cats are __________ . (he)

2 Choose the correct answers.

1 I love your drawing. Do you like **my** / **mine**?
2 Is this jacket **your** / **yours**?
3 Do you like **our** / **ours** house?
4 **Her** / **Hers** bike is better than his.
5 **Their** / **theirs** dog is very small.
6 **My** / **Mine** favourite hobby is playing the guitar.

Unit 12

Conjunctions *and*, *but*, *or*

His clothes are green **and** yellow.
I'm big **but** I'm not strong.
Are you tall **or** short?

1 Make sentences.

1 A zebra is a fast runner
2 A horse doesn't eat meat
3 A frog can be green, yellow, blue

A but it eats grass.
B or orange.
C and it's black and white.

2 Write *and*, *but* or *or*.

1 The lizard is small __________ green.
2 Tigers are scary __________ I like them.
3 It's a small butterfly __________ it's beautiful.
4 My cat is black __________ white.
5 Eva likes football __________ tennis.
6 Monsters can be happy __________ angry.
7 I'm not thirsty __________ I'm hungry.
8 Would you like an orange juice __________ an apple juice?

Unit 7

Would like + noun or verb

1 What would you like? Ask and answer with a friend.

a drink	talk to a robot
a crocodile	have a pet
a duck	sing a song
a motorbike	go to a zoo
a kite	ride a horse

Examples
– *Would you like a drink?*
– *Yes, I would.*
– *Would you like to talk to a robot?*
– *No, I wouldn't.*

Unit 1

Question words *what, how, who, how many*

Student A

2 Ask a friend questions about Eva. Use *what colour*, *how*, *how many* and *who*. Write the answers.

Example
A: *What's her name?*
B: *Her name's Eva.*

Name:	Sam
Eye colour:	blue
Brothers:	2
Sisters:	1
Best friend:	Anna
Goes to school:	by bus

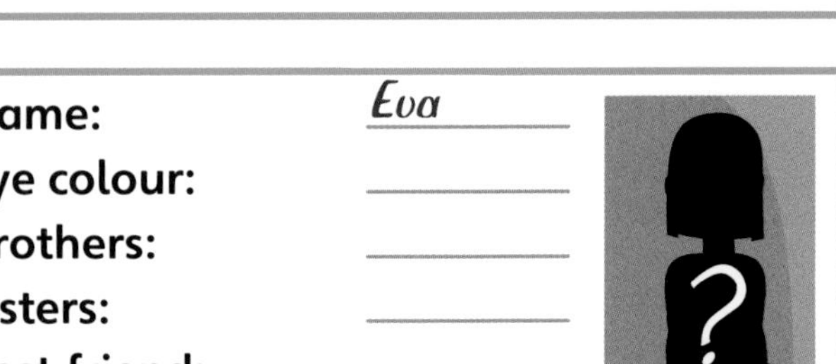

Name:	Eva
Eye colour:	
Brothers:	
Sisters:	
Best friend:	
Goes to school:	

Unit 3

Question word *where & prepositions of place*

Student A

3 Where are they? Ask a friend questions. Draw.

Listen to your friend and answer.
Ask about:

Piper
Frankie
Nedda

Examples
B: *Where is Piper?*
A: *He's in the garden. He's under the tree.*

Units 5 and 10

Determiners: *a, the, some*
Nouns: countable and uncountable

Student A

5 Tell a friend about the food.

Listen to your friend and draw.

Examples
A: *There's some orange juice.*

Grammar fun pairwork!

Unit 12

Conjunctions *and*, *but*, *or*

2 Add the conjunctions with a friend.

1 She's a good runner she can't swim.

____

2 He drinks orange juice apple juice for breakfast.

____

3 They like bears hippos.

____

Unit 1

Question words *what*, *how*, *who*, *how many*

Student B

3 Ask a friend questions about Sam. Use *what colour*, *how*, *how many* and *who*. Write the answers.

Examples B: *What's his name?*
A: *His name's Sam.*

Name:	Sam
Eye colour:	______
Brothers:	______
Sisters:	______
Best friend:	______
Goes to school:	______

Name:	Eva
Eye colour:	brown
Brothers:	1
Sisters:	1
Best friend:	Grace
Goes to school:	by car

Unit 3

Question word *where* & prepositions of place

Student B

4 Where are they? Ask a friend questions. Draw.

Listen to your friend and answer.
Ask about:

Max Frankie Nedda

Examples A: *Where is Max?*
B: *He's in the bedroom. He's on the bed.*

Units 5 and 10

Determiners: *a*, *the*, *some*
Nouns: countable and uncountable

Student B

5 Tell a friend about the food.

Listen to a friend and draw.

Examples B: *There's some lemonade.*

Reading & Writing Checklist

Circle if your answer is Yes!

My handwriting is clear and tidy. 

I don't have problems spelling English words. 

I can show if a word matches a picture by drawing a tick or a cross. 

I know and can spell more than five food words. 

I can answer questions about a picture with 'yes' or 'no'. 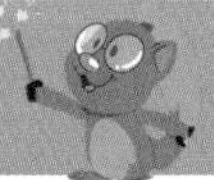

I can understand a short story with pictures. 

I know and can spell more than five words for things at the beach. 

I can write sentences about what people are doing. 

I know and can spell more than five words for things in the house. 

I can answer questions about a story by filling in gaps. 

I knew the words for all the things in Max's school bag in task 3 on page 7. 

I knew all the words in task 5 on page 9 and ticked and crossed the boxes correctly.

I wrote the sentences about the children in the park correctly in task 6 on page 11.

I wrote about me and my friend in task 4 on page 18.

I read the instructions and made a pop-up card in task 7 on page 19.

I unjumbled the words for places you see numbers in task 4 on page 29.

I wrote the correct words in the gaps in the text about frogs in task 4 on page 33.

I remember the six adjectives in task 3 on page 42 and I can spell them.

I wrote six sentences about the crocodile in task 4 on page 47.

I matched the sentences about the children on a school trip to the correct pictures in task 6 on page 57.

How many magic squirrels did you get?

Listening Checklist

Circle [squirrel] if your answer is Yes!

I can recognise lots of words I know when they are spoken in my book. 

I matched the names to the correct school bags in task 2 on page 6. 

I like matching names to a picture of people by drawing a line. 

I circled the correct answers about the alien in task 4 on page 23. 

I can understand and write the numbers 1–20 when I hear them. 

I pointed to the correct pictures of children in the house in task 6 on page 31. 

I can choose the correct picture when I hear it described. 

I put the pictures of the children in a café in the correct order in task 2 on page 38. 

I can colour a picture when I listen to a description. 

I circled the pictures with the correct colour in task 2 on page 64. 

How many magic squirrels did you get?

Speaking Checklist

Check your progress, colour the stars!	OK	Great
I can understand questions my teacher asks in English.	☆	☆☆
I asked and answered questions about what is in a school bag in task 5 on page 7.	☆	☆☆
I can talk about a picture using sentences, not just one word.	☆	☆☆
I talked with my friend about what we do on our birthdays in task 2 on page 16.	☆	☆☆
I can answer questions about pictures with short answers.	☆	☆☆
I described my tree house in task 3 on page 30.	☆	☆☆
I enjoyed acting out ordering a meal in a café in task 5 on page 39.	☆	☆☆
I can speak about myself and what I like doing.	☆	☆☆
I talked about the things I take to the beach in task 3 on page 52.	☆	☆☆
It's fun to speak English in class.	☆	☆☆

Word list

Unit 1

bag *n* ______________

blue *adj* ______________

classroom *n* ______________

colour *n* ______________

crayon *n* ______________

cupboard *n* ______________

desk *n* ______________

draw *v* ______________

green *adj* ______________

pen *n* ______________

photo *n* ______________

pink *adj* ______________

poster *n* ______________

purple *adj* ______________

read *v* ______________

ruler *n* ______________

school *n* ______________

talk *v* ______________

write *v* ______________

yellow *adj* ______________

Unit 2

ball *n* ______________

bat *n* ______________

bike *n* ______________

bird *n* ______________

boat *n* ______________

boots *n* ______________

brown *adj* ______________

camera *n* ______________

catch *v* ______________

clean *adj* ______________

crocodile *n* ______________

dirty *adj* ______________

dog *n* ______________

duck *n* ______________

eat *v* ______________

fish *n* ______________

flower *n* ______________

football *n* ______________

handbag *n* ______________

hit *v* ______________

hold *v* ______________

ice cream *n* ______________

kick *v* ______________

kite *n* ______________

monkey *n* ______________

paper *n* ______________

park *n* ______________

pick up *v* ______________

picture *n* ______________

ride *v* ______________

run *v* ______________

skateboard *n* ______________

sleep *v* ______________

snake *n* ______________

sun *n* ______________

throw *v* ______________

walk *v* ______________

water *n* ______________

Unit 3

balloon *n* ______________

birthday *n* ______________

cake *n* ______________

chair *n* ______________

clothes *n* ______________

open *v* ______________

robot *n* ______________

sing *v* ______________

song *n* ______________

toy *n* ______________

Unit 4

alien *n* ______________

beach *n* ______________

bear *n* ______________

bed *n* ______________

bedroom *n* ______________

black *adj* ______________

board game *n* ______________

book *n* ______________

bread *n* ______________

burger *n* ______________

ear *n* ______________

face *n* ______________

foot/feet *n* ______________

frog *n* ______________

giraffe *n* ______________

goat *n* ______________

grape *n* ______________

happy *adj* ______________

horse *n* ______________

lemon *n* ______________

lemonade *n* ______________

lizard *n* ______________

mango *n* ______________

monster *n* ______________

onion *n* ______________

orange *adj* ______________

paint *v* ______________

pea *n* ______________

pear *n* ______________

pineapple *n* ______________

plane *n* ______________

playground *n* ______________

sad *adj* ______________

sand *n* ______________

sea *n* ______________

shop *n* ____________

skateboarding *n* ____________

smile *n* ____________

spider *n* ____________

sweet(s) *n* ____________

tail *n* ____________

train *n* ____________

TV *n* ____________

watermelon *n* ____________

white *adj* ____________

zoo *n* ____________

Unit 5

banana *n* ____________

bookshop *n* ____________

bus *n* ____________

chicken *n* ____________

chocolate *n* ____________

clock *n* ____________

close *v* ____________

computer *n* ____________

doll *n* ____________

door *n* ____________

egg *n* ____________

glasses *n* ____________

grandma *n* ____________

hat *n* ____________

house *n* ____________

jacket *n* ____________

jeans *n* ____________

kiwi *n* ____________

lime *n* ____________

meatballs *n* ____________

nose *n* ____________

pie *n* ____________

potato *n* ____________

sock *n* ____________

street *n* ____________

teacher *n* ____________

teddy (bear) *n* ____________

tomato *n* ____________

T-shirt *n* ____________

Unit 6

armchair *n* ____________

bathroom *n* ____________

dinner *n* ____________

guitar *n* ____________

jellyfish *n* ____________

kitchen *n* ____________

mirror *n* ____________

piano *n* ____________

polar bear *n* ____________

scary *adj* ____________

tree *n* ____________

wall *n* ____________

Unit 7

breakfast *n* ____________

carrot *n* ____________

coconut *n* ____________

juice *n* ____________

lunch *n* ____________

orange *n* ____________

rice *n* ____________

Unit 8

baseball *n* ____________

basketball *n* ____________

cat *n* ____________

clap *v* ____________

sheep *n* ____________

shorts *n* ____________

tennis *n* ____________

window *n* ____________

Unit 9

elephant *n* ____________

fly *v* ____________

hippo *n* ____________

jump *v* ____________

shoe *n* ____________

swim *v* ____________

tiger *n* ____________

zebra *n* ____________

Unit 10

apple *n* ____________

baseball cap *n* ____________

shell *n* ____________

ship *n* ____________

Unit 11

car *n* ____________

cow *n* ____________

pencil *n* ____________

phone *n* ____________

sit *v* ____________

tablet *n* ____________

watch *n* ____________

Unit 12

hand *n* ____________

keyboard (computer) *n* ____________

mouse (computer) *n* ____________

sofa *n* ____________

In your book ...

Likes: puppies, videos, drawing, spaghetti, the moon, unicorns

Dislikes: sharks, lions, aliens, broccoli

Likes: sports, snow, skating, caves

Dislikes: water, dancing, umbrellas

Likes: carrot, music, eggs, apples, running, dancing, pears, grapes

Dislikes: candy, riding bikes, lettuce, oranges

Likes: friends, gum

Dislikes: blood, scary things

Likes: flying, reading stories

Dislikes: walking, hats, boots

Likes: fashion, pink, bed, hugs

Dislikes: soup

... from kids around the world

Alejandra, 8

Hugo, 8

Julia, 8

Luíza, 7

Alan, 6

Anna, 7

Jesse

Likes: flying, burritos, spiders, dancing, red, eating

Dislikes: mushrooms, yellow, cats, black

Checklist buddy

Likes: pizza, apple juice, playing ball

Dislikes: ice cream, burgers, mice, cats

Exam Professor

Likes: science, music, interesting animals, playing basketball

Dislikes: disorder, meat, destruction, black

Max

Likes: balloons, bananas, apples

Dislikes: cleaning my room

Think Big Giraffe

Likes: plants

Dislikes: meat

Sage

Likes: reading, eating, joking, art

Dislikes: pickles, flies, the dark, cockroaches

Aurora, 9

Luisa, 7

Mariya, 8

Mario, 11

Adriana, 7

Edith, 11

Author acknowledgements

Claire Medwell would like to give thanks to the editorial team for all their help and support throughout the writing process and to her children who provide an endless source of inspiration. She would also like to give special thanks to Matthew English from IH Reggio Calabria, Italy for his inspiring ideas on using Art in the YL's classroom.

Montse Watkin would like to acknowledge all the inspiring colleagues she has had the pleasure of working with over the years.

Publisher acknowledgements

The authors and publishers are grateful to the following for reviewing the material during the writing process:

Jane Ritter, Georgia Forte: Italy; Angela McFarland: Vietnam; Maritza Suarez Gonzalez: Mexico; Muruvvet Celik: Turkey; Roisin O'Farrell: Spain.

Acknowledgements

The authors and publishers acknowledge the following sources of copyright material and are grateful for the permissions granted. While every effort has been made, it has not always been possible to identify the sources of all the material used, or to trace all copyright holders. If any omissions are brought to our notice, we will be happy to include the appropriate acknowledgements on reprinting & in the next update to the digital edition, as applicable.

Key: GR: Grammar; Rev: Review unit; U: Unit

Photography

All photographs are sourced from Getty Images.

GR: Jamie Grill/The Image Bank; Seseg Zhigzhitova/EyeEm; Philippe Desnerck/Photolibrary; Esther Moreno Martinez/EyeEm; PeopleImages/E+; Vadmary/iStock/Getty Images Plus; GILKIS - Emielke van Wyk/GILKIS - Emielke van Wyk; fmajor/iStock Unreleased; mediaphotos/iStock/Getty Images Plus; Rev: Jonas Gratzer/LightRocket; Creative Crop/DigitalVision; PhotoObjects.net/Getty Images Plus; PetrBonek/iStock/Getty Images Plus; Dan Thornberg/EyeEm; Ales-A/E+; Blend Images - Kris Timken; Brighton Dog Photography/Moment; Praveenkumar Palanichamy/Moment; Dorling Kindersley; Compassionate Eye Foundation/Rob Daly/OJO Images Ltd/Photodisc; Hero Images; Marc Romanelli; Asia Images Group; kupicoo/E+; SensorSpot/E+; Hill Street Studios/DigitalVision; Marcus Lyon/Photographer's Choice; Glow Images, Inc/Glow; fotosipsak/E+; Fuse/Corbis; kali9/E+; xefstock/E+; andresr/E+; Tang Ming Tung/Photodisc; **U1:** artisteer/iStock/Getty Images Plus; Will Heap/Dorling Kindersley; Stefano Cremisini/EyeEm; targovcom/iStock/Getty Images Plus; DAJ; Suparat Malipoom/EyeEm; epicurean/E+; HECTOR RETAMAL/AFP; Chau Doan/LightRocket; FatCam[illegible]/E+; Juanmonino/iStock/Getty Images Plus; Andersen Ro[illegible]otography Inc/DigitalVision; Juanmonino/E+; Johnny[illegible]/E+; eskaylim/iStock/Getty Images Plus; Andy Crawf[illegible]orling Kindersley; **U2:** Glow Images; JGI/Jamie Grill; J[illegible]s O'Neil/DigitalVision; itsabreeze photography/Moment; DE[illegible] ROMANO/De Agostini; **U3:** Mike Powell/Photodisc; Abhishe[illegible]akur/EyeEm; Best View Stock; gpointstudio/iStock/Getty I[illegible]ges Plus; Colin Hawkins/Cultura; From Hurricane1984/Momen[illegible] PhotoAlto/Sigrid Olsson/PhotoAlto Agency RF Collecti[illegible]ns; Granger Wootz; Tang Ming Tung/Photodisc; **U4:** roevin/Moment; Stephen Oliver/Dorling Kindersley; Sharon White/Photographer's Choice; Dorling Kindersley: Charlotte Tolhurst; Yevgen Romanenko/Moment; Ronald Leunis/EyeEm; Jose A. Bernat Bacete/Moment; JohnnyGreig/E+; Maximilian Stock Ltd./Photolibrary; Paul Biris/Moment Open; Erich Karnberger/iStock/Getty Images Plus; devolmon/iStock/Getty Images Plus; Steve Debenport/E+; **U5:** Ng Sok Lian/EyeEm; Andy Crawford/Dorling Kindersley; Photo credit John Dreyer/Moment Open; Fotonen/iStock/Getty Images Plus; Yevgen Romanenko/Moment; Gary Ombler and Andy Crawford/Dorling Kindersley; Olga Gillmeister/iStock/Getty Images Plus; DustyPixel/E+; SabrinaPintus/iStock/Getty Images Plus; AleksandarGeorgiev/E+; Alexandre Macieira/EyeEm; lovelypeace/iStock/Getty Images Plus; Tom Craig/Photolibrary; Thomas Kline/Design Pics/Perspectives; Enes Evren/iStock/Getty Images Plus; chas53/iStock/Getty Images Plus; Anadolu Agency; Isabel Pavia/Moment Open; Esthermm/Moment; MoreISO/iStock Editorial/Getty Images Plus; michaelpuche/iStock/Getty Images Plus; Vstock LLC/VStock; Jessica Nelson/Moment Open; peepo/E+; **U6:** romana chapman/Moment; Â© Hiya Images/Corbis; PeopleImages/iStock/Getty Images Plus; Rawpixel/iStock/Getty Images Plus; sl-f/iStock/Getty Images Plus; Ed Freeman/Stone; David Santiago Garcia/Aurora; Vicki Jauron, Babylon and Beyond Photography/Moment; U7: Lina Moiseienko/iStock/Getty Images Plus; Kondor83/iStock/Getty Images Plus; Jose A. Bernat Bacete/Moment; Adisak Lapwutirat/EyeEm; Kemi H Photography/Moment Open; kiankhoon/iStock/Getty Images Plus; Education Images/Universal Images Group; Hero Images; istetiana/Moment; **U8:** FatCamera/E+; GraphicaArtis/Archive Photos; DEA/G. DAGLI ORTI; Universal History Archive/Universal Images Group; Gearstd/iStock/Getty Images Plus; Classen Rafael/EyeEm; Photo 12/Universal Images Group; U9: DLILLC/Corbis/VCG/Corbis Documentary; Richard Wager/Moment; The world is a beautiful place, there's beauty in everything/Moment; Paul Starosta/Corbis Documentary; Darrell Gulin/Photographer's Choice; Jose A. Bernat Bacete/Moment; Barcroft Media; ullstein bild; Ole Jorgen Liodden/naturepl.com/Nature Picture Library; Douglas Sacha/Moment; Martin Harvey/Gallo Images; JGI/Jamie Grill; **U10:** Charriau Pierre/The Image Bank; Stephen Knowles Photography/Moment; roevin/Moment; Westend61; Sergei Malgavko/TASS; joingate/iStock/Getty Images Plus; Dan Prince/Cultura; Arterra/Universal Images Group; **U11:** Westend61; Leland Bobbe/DigitalVision; andresr/E+; FatCamera/E+; xefstock/E+; Fotoatelier Berlin/imageBROKER; Yvette Cardozo/The Image Bank; kali9/iStock/Getty Images Plus; THEPALMER/E+; Mike Tauber; Meg Takamura; Marcy Maloy/Photodisc; **U12:** Shin Taro/Moment; PeopleImages/E+; Portra Images/Taxi; Wavebreakmedia/iStock/Getty Images Plus; Ariel Skelley/DigitalVision; Jose Luis Pelaez Inc/DigitalVision; Emrah Turudu/Photographer's Choice RF.

The following photograph is sourced from another library.
U8: Keith Haring artwork and writing © Keith Haring Foundation

Illustrations

Pablo Gallego (Beehive); Dave Williams (Bright); Leo Trinidad (Bright); Fran Brylewska (Beehive); Amanda Enright (Advocate); Collaborate Agency, Wild Apple Design Ltd.

Front cover illustrations by Amanda Enright; Leo Trinidad; Jhonny Nunez; Pol Cunyat; Benedetta Capriotti; Dan Widdowson; Pand P Studio/Shutterstock; Piotr Urakau/Shutterstock.

Audio

Audio production by Ian Harker

Song and chants composition and production by AmyJo Doherty and Martin Spangle.

Design

Design and typeset by Wild Apple Design Ltd

Cover design by Collaborate agency

Additional design layout EMC design Ltd

FUN Skills

Home Booklet 2

Montse Watkin

Reading

A B C D E

Alice	Mark	Ben	May	Kim

Hi. I'm Mark and this is my young brother.

I'm May. I'm on my bike in front of my sister.

Hello. I'm Alice. I'm a grandmother with my family.

My name's Ben. I'm in between my two sisters.

Hi there. Who am I?

Read and look. Match the names to the people in the photos.

Fun boost

How many girls' names can you write in one minute?

How many boys' names can you write in one minute?

Ask your family to time you.

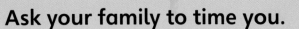

Maria, Sofia, ____________

____

Paolo, Danny, ____________

____

____

Reading

Look at the code. Write the four presents the children are taking to the party. Colour the objects in the balloon.

I've got some purple

1 _ _ _ _ _ _ _ _ .

I've got a red

2 _ _ _ _ _ .

I'm taking some pink

3 _ _ _ _ _ _ _ .

I'm taking some yellow

4 _ _ _ _ _ .

Fun boost

Look at the letters again. Draw the code for:

Example

a fruit 

1 a colour

2 a part of the body

3 a number

Reading

❶ **Complete the crossword.**

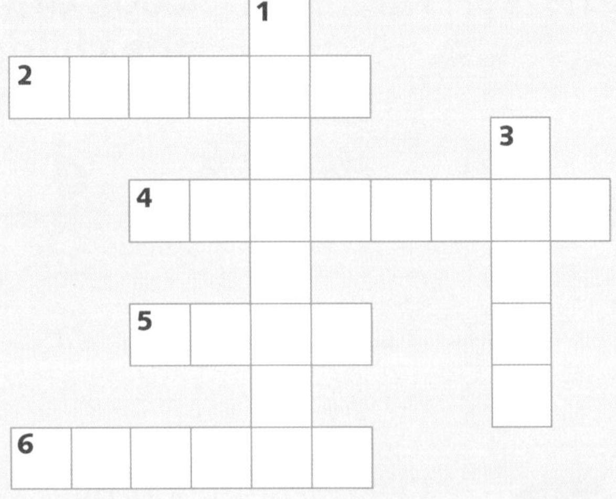

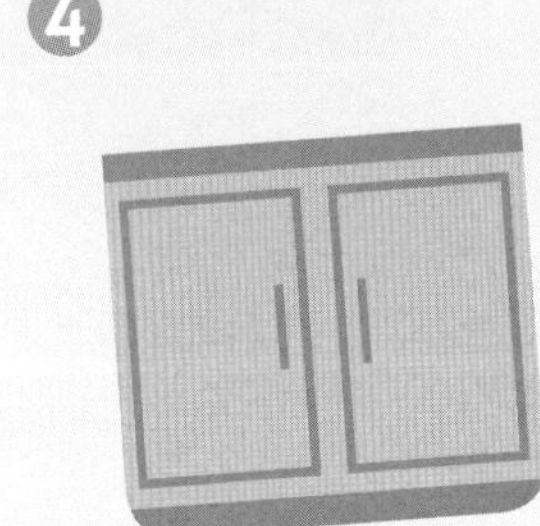

❷ **Look and read. Put a tick (✓) or a cross (✗) in the box.**

1 This has got a keyboard. ☐

2 These live in your garden. ☐

3 These have got leaves. ☐

4 This is for your clothes. ☐

5 This swims in the sea. ☐

6 This has got eight legs. ☐

Fun boost

Learn a magic trick to surprise your friends!

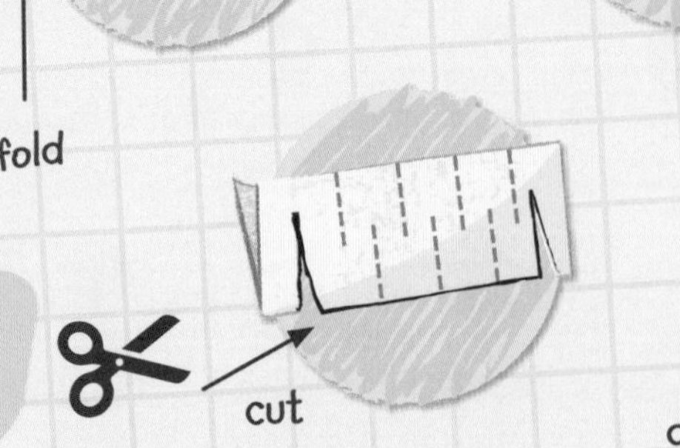

1 Fold a big piece of paper.

2 Cut lines on two sides.

3 Cut along the folded edge. Don't cut the two folded ends.

4 Open your paper. Walk through it!

Reading

Look at the picture. Read and draw lines to answer *yes* or *no*.

YES

NO

Example The monkey is happy.

1 Two ducks are swimming on the water.

2 Two dogs are running and playing.

3 There are three children in the park.

4 A boy is flying a kite.

5 Two girls are skateboarding.

Fun boost

Design your own park!

1 Decorate your box.

2 Make some paper or playdough children or animals.

3 Put them in your box.

4 Talk about your park.

Reading

Read. Write the correct words below.

Giraffes live in Africa. They have a very long neck and four long legs. This helps them to eat the leaves of tall trees. Giraffes don't drink water every day. They get water from the leaves they eat.
You can see giraffes and zebras living together. But giraffes don't like lions or crocodiles!

Giraffes

place	______________________
body	long neck and long ______________
food	leaves from ______________
drink	______________________
who they like ...	______________________
who they don't like ...	______________ and ______________

Fun boost

Make a giraffe!

1 **Draw the parts of the giraffe on cardboard.**

2 **Cut out. (Be careful with scissors.)**

3 **Put it together!**

Reading

Read the story. Write the missing words.

Weeee, this is fun!

Monkey has a surprise for his three friends.
Monkey says, 'Come with me!'
But Elephant says, 'I can't, I'm having my **1** ________ !'
Giraffe says, 'Not now, I'm having my **2** ________ .'
Tiger says, 'Shh, I'm sleeping in my **3** ________ !'

Monkey is sad, but he climbs a **4** ________ and ...
flies across the jungle!

Now Monkey's **5** ________ want to fly across the jungle too.
But it's night time.
Monkey says, 'It's OK! We can all go in the morning!'
Everyone is happy!

Fun boost

Look at the funny animal!
What can you see?

This animal has got an elephant's nose and ... ________

____

____

____

Invent and draw your own funny animal!

Listening

02 **Who are Nedda's friends? Listen and write the names.**

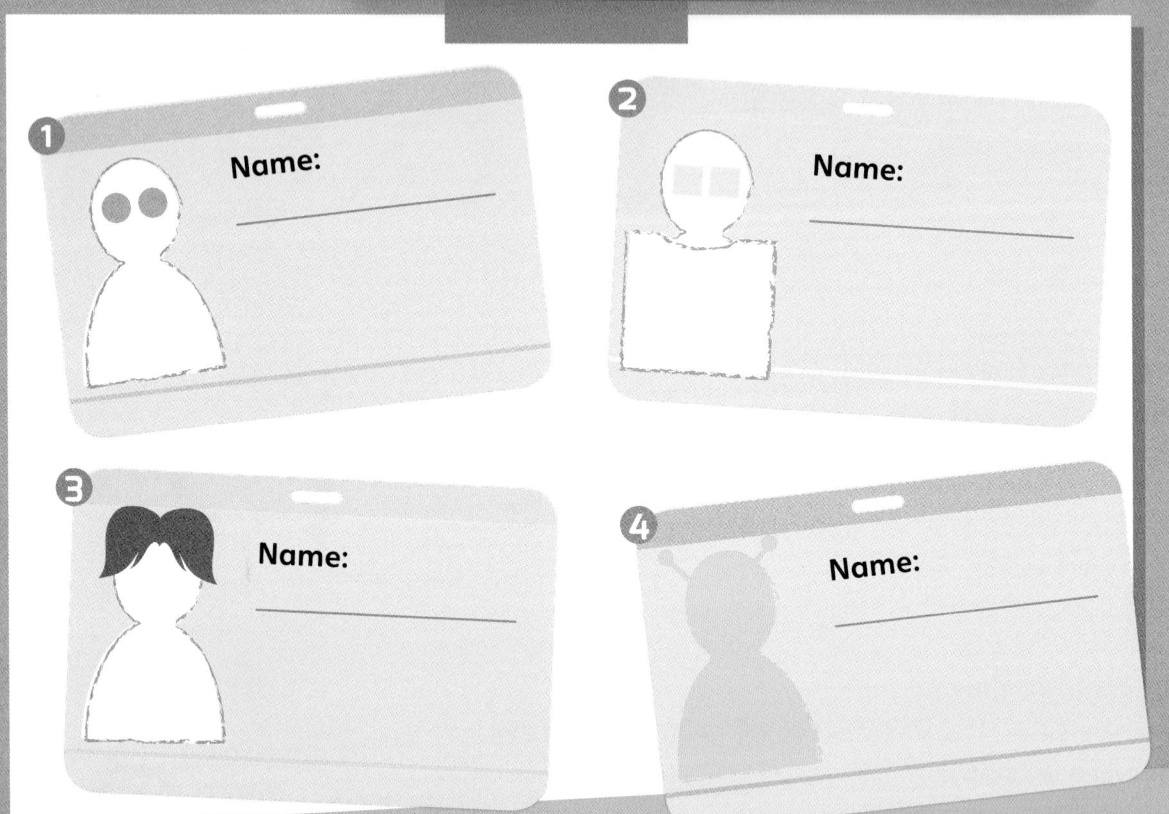

Fun boost

Write an acrostic poem.

1 Write your name.

2 Use the letters to write things you like.

3 Now write a poem with your name!

I like ...

Trains
Oranges
Music

I like ...

Sweets
Apples
Robots
Animals

Listening

❶ 03 Listen and write the numbers.

❷ Draw the missing dots.
Now circle the winner, A or B.

Fun boost

Do the number quiz! Find the answers.

What 5 sports have a ball?

In the supermarket, you can buy boxes of ? eggs or 12 eggs.

What is the word for '100' in English?

What 3 countries begin with C?

Has a bee got 2 wings or 4 wings?

Are there 7 or 8 colours in a rainbow?

Have you got 20 teeth?

What 2 animals have 8 legs?

Listening

04 **Look at the pictures. Listen and tick (✓) the box.**

1 Where does Mark live?

A ☐ B ☐ C ☐

2 What does Grace eat at the party?

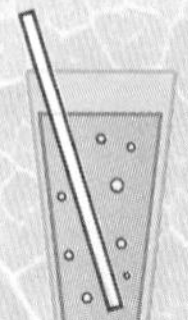

A ☐ B ☐ C ☐

3 What is Mark's present from his parents?

A ☐ B ☐ C ☐

4 Where do the children play?

A ☐ B ☐ C ☐

Fun boost

Do this party trick with your friends and family!

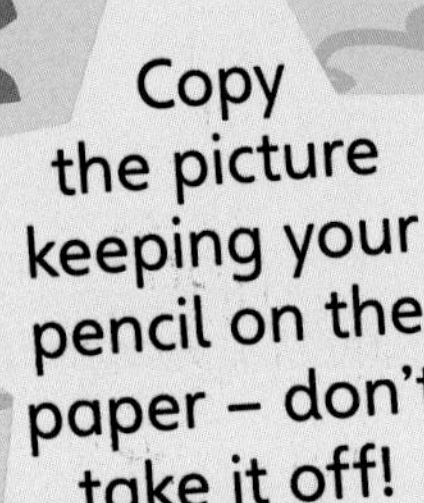

Copy the picture keeping your pencil on the paper – don't take it off!

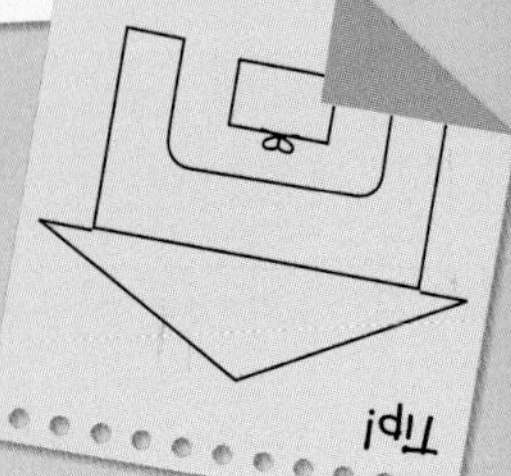

Listening

05 **Look at the park. Listen and colour.**

Fun boost

Make magic milk!

1 Add milk to a dish.
2 Add food colouring.
3 Add washing-up liquid on a cotton bud.
4 Watch the magic!

Writing

1

Read the clues. Look at the paintings. Write the words.

1 You can ride in this (**painting 2**).

_ _ _ _

(o t a b)

2 A man is playing this (**painting 3**).

_ _ _ _ _ _

(t a r i g u)

3 This is behind the table and chair (**painting 1**).

_ _ _ _ _ _

(o d w w n i)

4 This is big and brown (**painting 4**).

_ _ _ _

(e t r e)

5 This is red and in a woman's hair (**painting 3**).

_ _ _ _ _ _

(w e r o l f)

6 This is next to the sea (**painting 2**).

_ _ _ _ _ _

(e b c a h)

2

3

4

Fun boost

Look at the painting. Count and write the number. I can see …

________ heads. ________ feet.

________ hands. ________ bodies.

Writing

Look at the pictures and letters. Read and write the words.

One arm is a _ _ _ _ _ _ .
Three arms are _ _ _ _ _ _ _ .
One head is a _ _ _ _ _ _ _ .
One body is a _ _ _ _ _ _ .

One leg is an _ _ _ _ _ .
Two legs are _ _ _ _ .
The hair is _ _ _ _ _ _ .
One nose is a _ _ _ _ _ _ .

Fun boost

Make a vegetable print picture.

1 Take a hard fruit or vegetable, like a potato.
2 Cut the fruit or vegetable in half.
3 Cut a nice shape like a heart, flower or face.
4 Paint one half.
5 Print on paper.

Writing

1 Find and circle eight words. Write them beside the correct double letters.

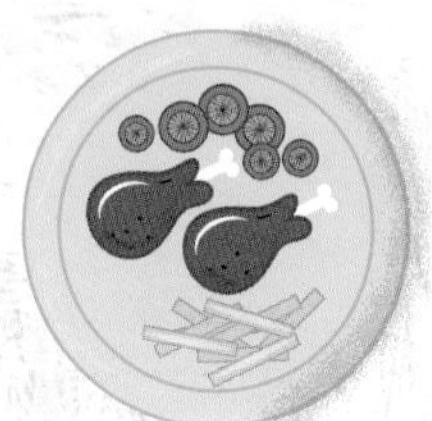

ee s h e e p   nn _ _ _ _ _ _

oo _ _ _ _ _   pp _ _ _ _ _

dd _ _ _ _ _   rr _ _ _ _ _ _

ll _ _ _ _ _   ss _ _ _ _ _ _ _

2 Look at the double letters above. Write more words like this.

Fun boost

Label things in your house!

Writing

a b j ea ch s ll p m n t

Use the code. Write the words.

I like …

playing on the _ _ _ _ _ .

wearing _ _ _ _ _ .

swimming in the _ _ _ .

eating _ _ _ _ _ _ _ _ _ .

I don't like …

eating _ _ _ _ _ .

Fun boost

Circle nine action words. Then mime them for your family!

Now make your own circle of words!

Writing

Luke

Cara

Finn

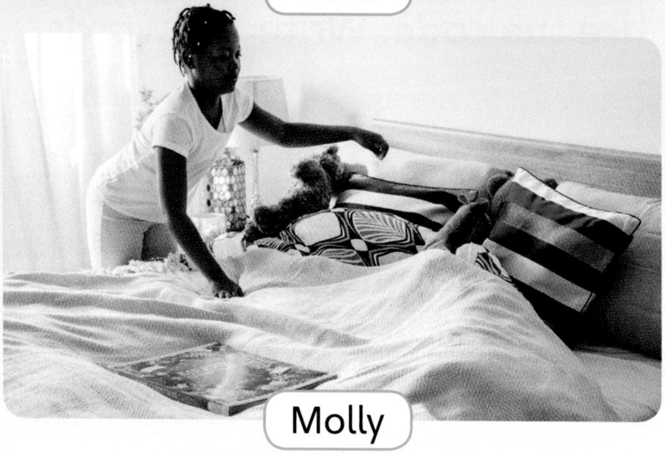

Molly

Look and read. Write *yes* or *no*.

1 Finn is on the floor. ________

2 There is a door behind Luke. ________

3 Molly is in the bathroom. ________

4 Cara is putting things on the table. ________

5 Finn is reading a book. ________

6 Luke is cleaning. ________

Fun boost

Make a fun bookmark!

1 Cut, fold and glue.

2 Make a funny face.

3 Put it on a page in your book.

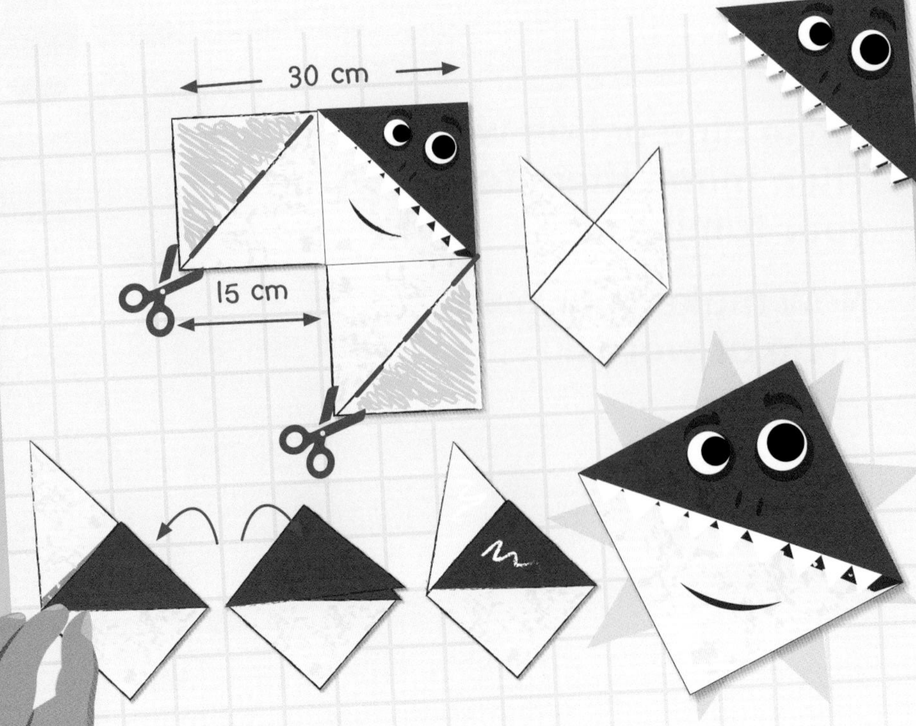

Writing

1 Put the words in order and complete the questions.

1 you / glasses / wearing

Are ______________________________ ?

2 school bag / got / you / a / blue

Have ______________________________ ?

3 swim / you

Can ______________________________ ?

4 a / you / flat / live / in

Do ______________________________ ?

5 food / your / pineapple / favourite

Is ______________________________ ?

2 Colour and match the answers.

Yes, I do.

No, it isn't.

No, I'm not.

Yes, I can.

No, I haven't.

Fun boost

Make a question wheel!

1 Cut out one big and one small circle.

2 Put them together.

3 Write *Have you got ...?*

4 Write names of people, pets or things.

Ask your questions!

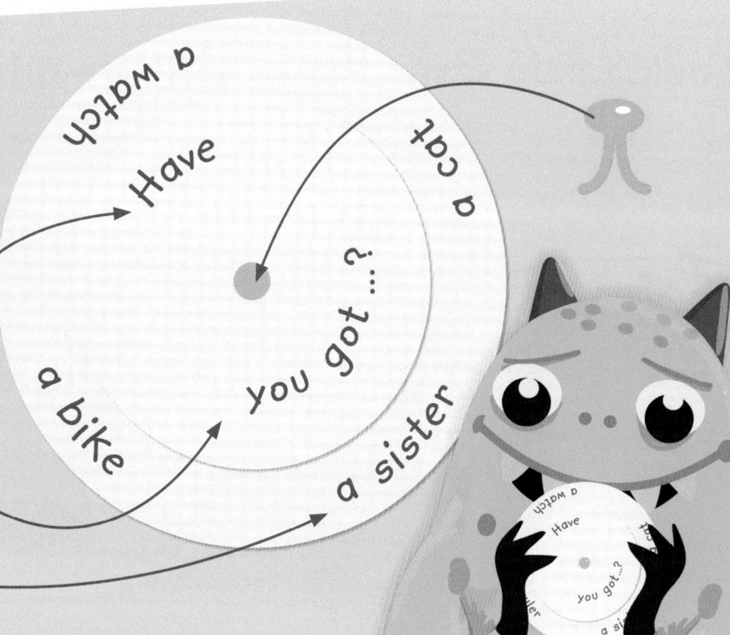

Writing

Look at the picture. Answer the questions.

1 Where is the woman?
on the ____________

2 What has the man got in his hand?
a ____________

3 How many children are there?
____

4 What pet have the family got?
____

5 Where is the girl sitting?
on the ____________

6 Who is singing?
the ____________

Fun boost

Look. Circle seven things that are different!

Writing

Cara's bedroom

Finn's bedroom

Molly's bedroom

Look at the bedrooms. Answer the questions.

1 What is behind the toy box?
a ________

2 How many robots are there?
____

3 What animal is on the computer and the table?
a ________

4 What is between the shoes?
a ________

5 Who plays the guitar?
____

6 Where are the shirts?
in the ________

Fun boost

Make an egg head!

1 Eat an egg.
2 Put cotton wool in the shell.
3 Add seeds and a little water.
4 Draw a face.
5 Put it next to your bedroom window.
6 Watch the hair grow!

mustard seeds

cotton wool

Speaking

1 **Look. Find these things in Picture A. Tick (✓) the box.**

2 06 **Then listen and move the things to Picture B. Draw lines.**

3 **Now tell your family where the things are.**

Fun boost

Read and say the sentences. What is it? Investigate!

It's a big, grey fish with lots of teeth.

It's a tall bird with long legs. It doesn't fly.

It's a house you make on the beach with sand.

It's a small animal that lives in a shell.

It's a boat that goes under the sea.

It's a place where lions and giraffes live.

Speaking

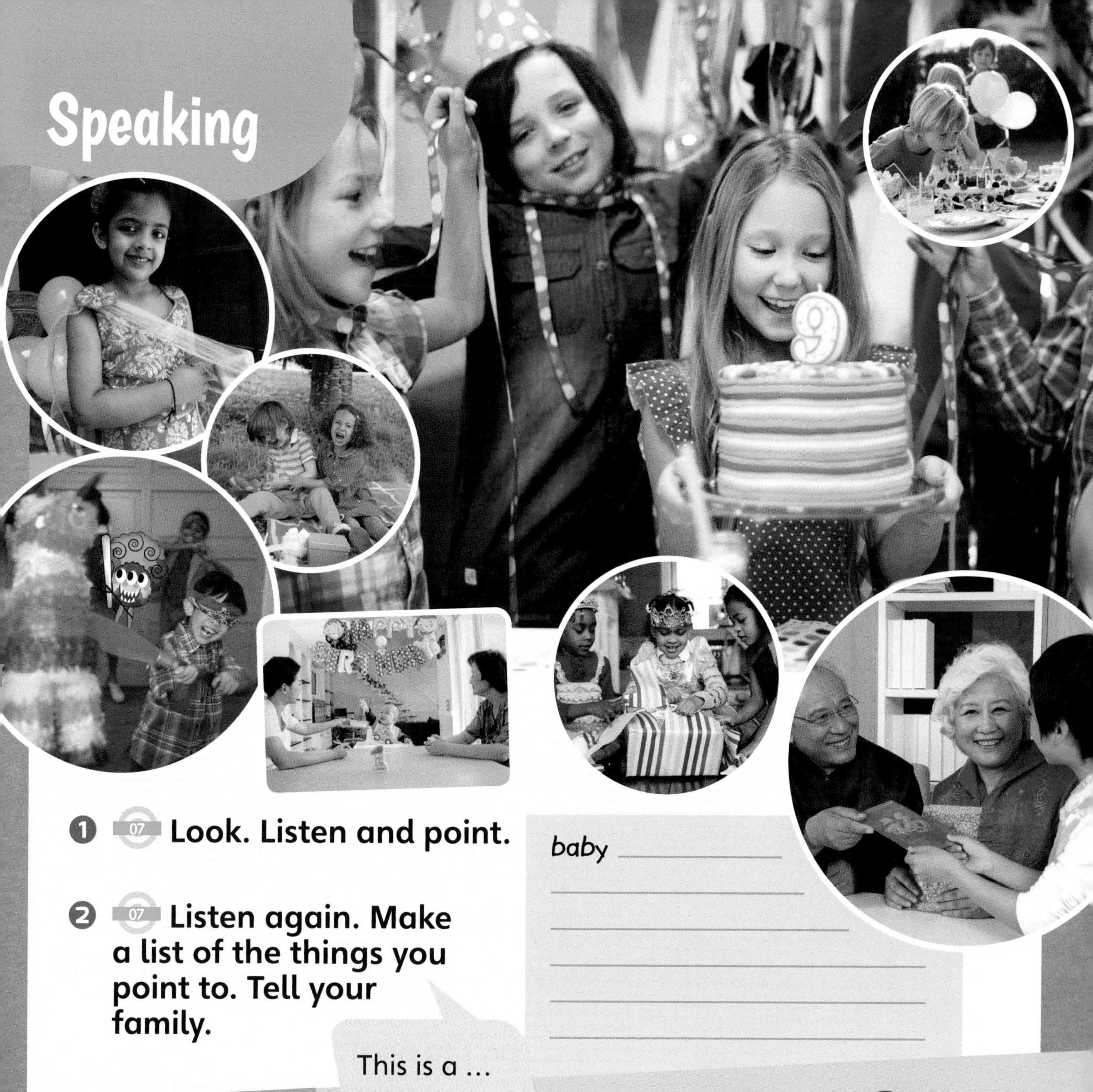

1 07 Look. Listen and point.

2 07 Listen again. Make a list of the things you point to. Tell your family.

This is a …

baby ___________

____

____

____

____

____

Fun boost

Do a birthday-present crossword!

Now stand in your bedroom. Call out the names of all the toys you see.

1			2				
			3				4
5							

Speaking

❶ **Look at the pictures 1–5 and answer the questions. Then cut out the cards on page 31.**

1 What's this? a _ _ _ _

2 What's this? a _ _ _ _

3 What's this? a _ _ _ _ castle

4 What's this? a _ _ _ _

5 What's this? a _ _ _ _ _ _

❷ 08 **Listen and put your cards on the photos.**

Fun boost

Which one is different? Say the name and circle it!

car sand beach sea

train skateboard bus plane

window sofa chair bed

ruler crayon rubber bag

Speaking

❶ 09 Listen and look at your object cards.
Now listen and answer the questions.

❷ Ask your family some questions.

Fun boost

**Find and count the objects.
Write the number.**

- 2 burgers
- ☐ crayons
- ☐ crocodiles
- ☐ giraffes
- ☐ hippos
- ☐ horses
- ☐ ice creams
- ☐ lemonades
- ☐ lizards
- ☐ pears

Now cover the picture. Say the number of things you remember.

A rainbow visit

10 I don't like walking or riding a bike. I like flying!

I fly to the park and I fly to school.

Today I'm flying to see my friend Bobbie.

He lives next to a rainbow.

I love visiting him. He eats silly, fun food.

Look! Rainbow cake and rainbow fruit! Fun-tastic!

What fruit can you see in Jesse's rainbow? Write a list.

Zoom the superhero!

11 A girl sends Zoom a message from her phone.

'Help us. A scary pirate is near our school.'

Zoom the superhero flies to the pirate ship.

The pirate is sad and says, 'People think I'm scary!'

Zoom says,'Let's visit the school and talk about your sea stories.'

The children love the funny stories.

The pirate is happy.

Draw a sea monster for one of the pirate's stories.

What Bobbie likes

12 I'm Bo**bb**ie and my favourite colours are gr**ee**n and ye**ll**ow.

I eat pinea**pp**les. I don't eat mangoes.

I have e**gg**s for breakfast, but not bread.

I like b**ee**s and tr**ee**s, but not spiders or flowers.

I play te**nn**is, but not badminton.

Do you know why I like these things?

Look at my name!

Write three more things Bobbie likes.

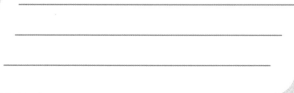

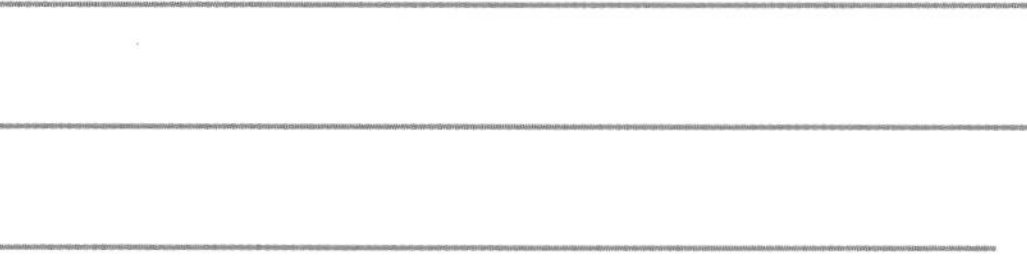

Nedda and the alien

13 Nedda's best friend on the moon is an alien. His name is Zak. He has a green head and body.

He doesn't walk; he flies on his skateboard.

He doesn't speak English; he speaks *Moonglish*!

Nedda is learning *Moonglish*.

Zak is a good teacher. He paints lots of pictures to help her!

Moonglish
hello = *babla*

Hello = ___________

Hello = ___________

Write the word *hello* in two different languages.

Piper's favourite food

14 Some bats eat fruit …

Urgh!

… and some bats eat insects.

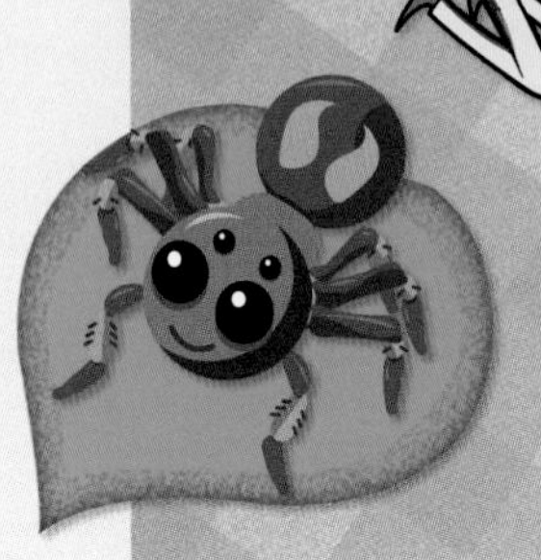

But Piper eats cake!

He loves chocolate cake, ice-cream cake, strawberry cake and birthday cake.

Urgh!

Mmm …

Where's the cake?

Draw a cake for Piper!

Detective Leon wants a new home!

Welcome to my house. It's in a tree!

It's fantastic and cool. You can see lots of things.

But …

… it's cold at night.

And …

… monkeys eat my food.

And …

… bats fly in my bedroom. I can't sleep!

But …

… I'm a detective and now I'm looking for a new home!

Leon

A very special detective.
I can find anything!
My phone number is

111 7793

Draw a cool garden for this house.

Frankie's new bag

Frankie loves bags!

She has got a handbag,
a beach bag and a school bag.

One day in the park, Frankie sees a girl.
She is throwing rubbish on the grass.
Frankie is sad, but she has an idea.

Now she has a rubbish bag, too
… and a new helper!

What rubbish goes in these bins? Draw one thing in each bin.

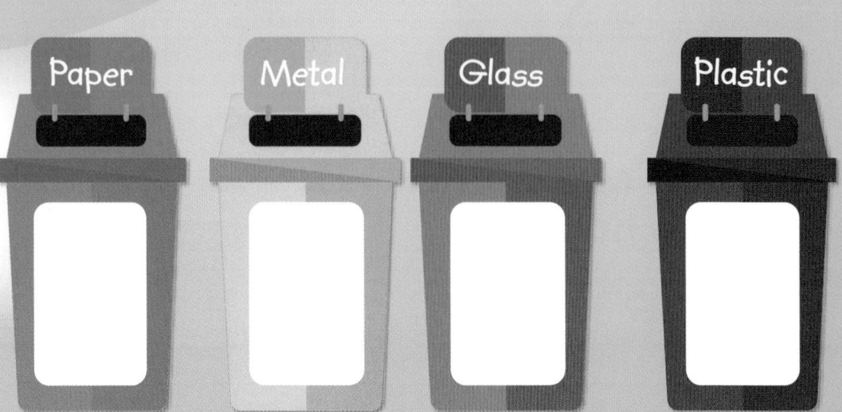

Object cards

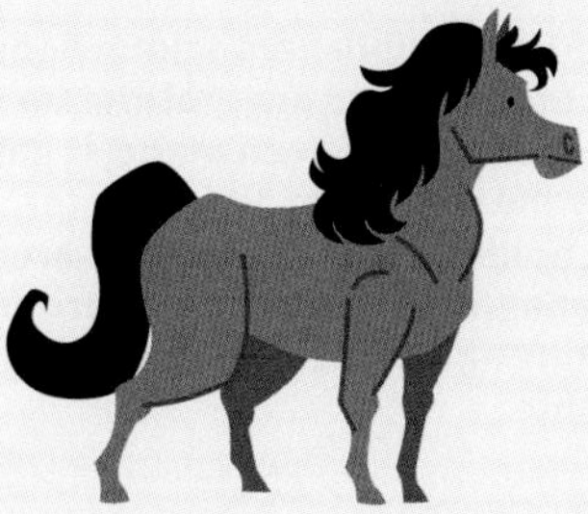

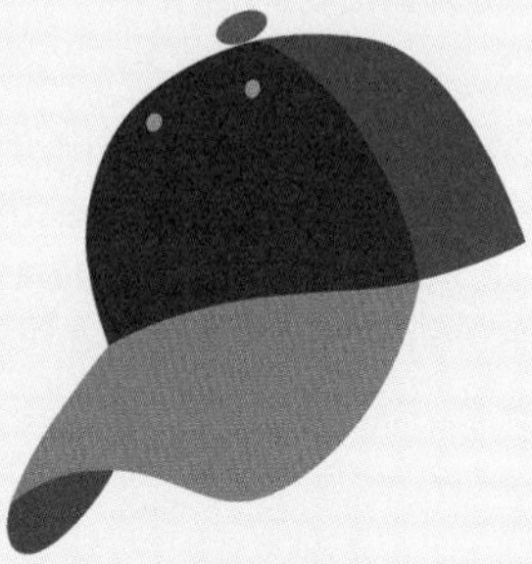

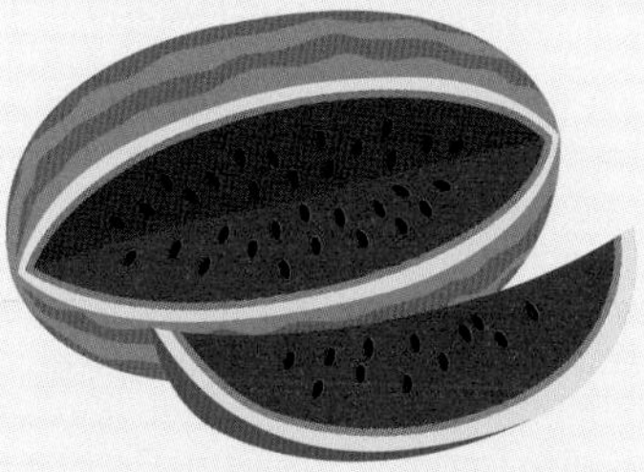

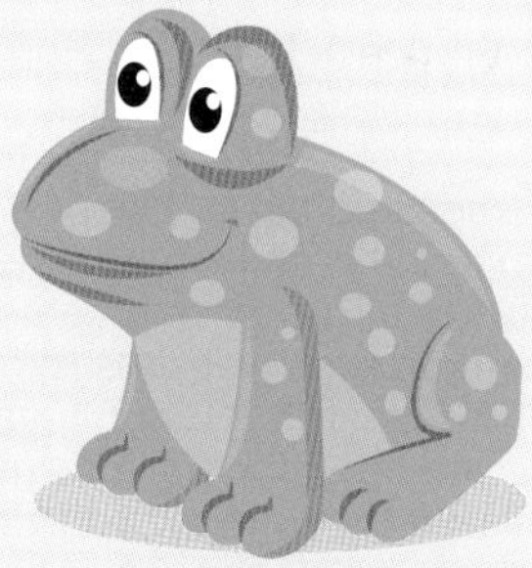

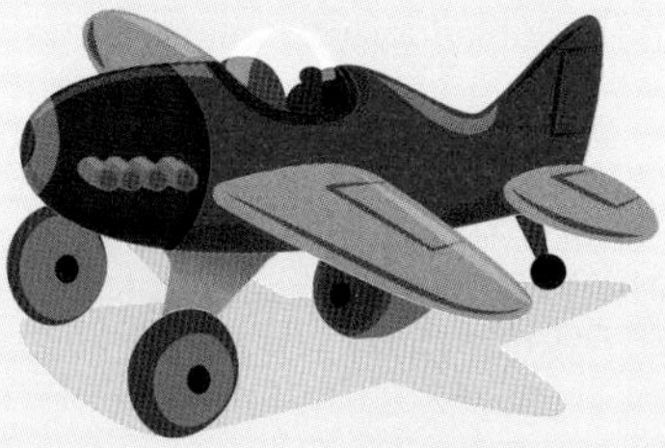

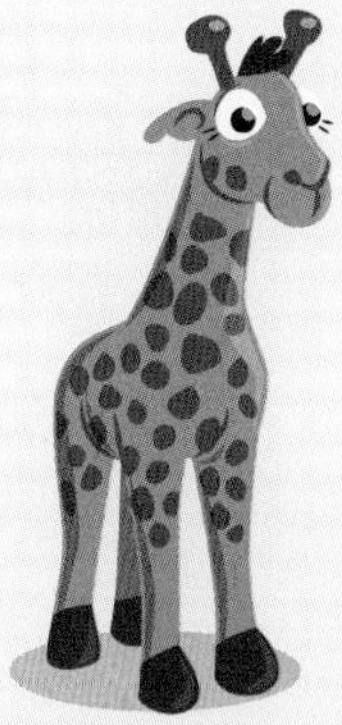

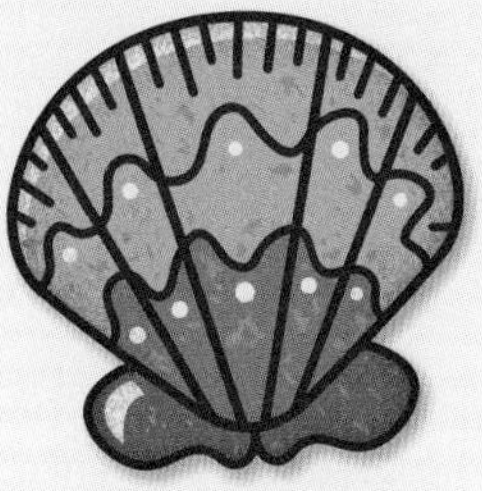

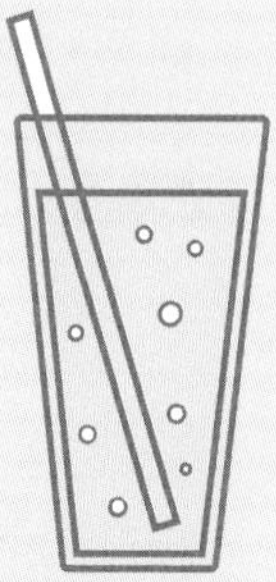

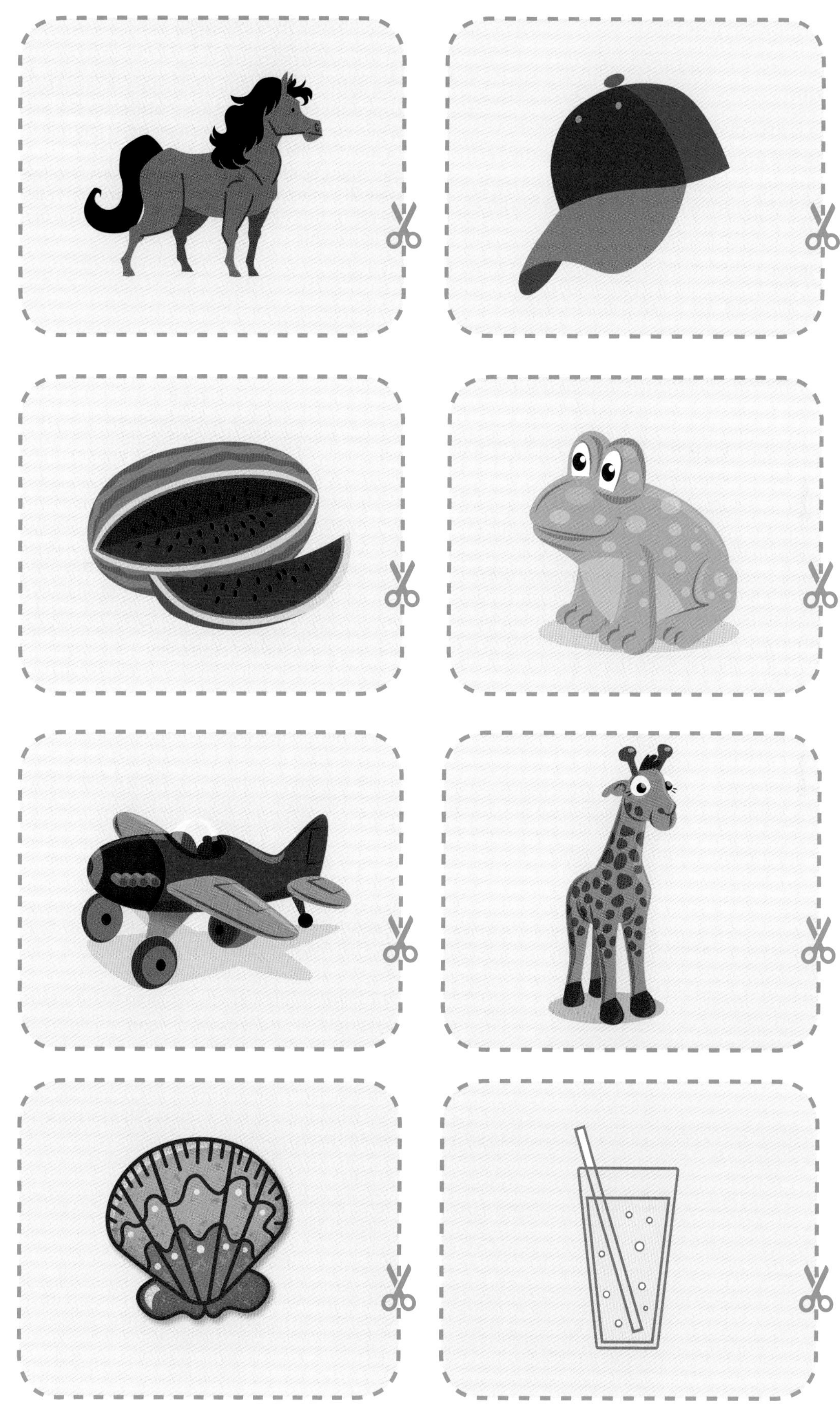

Cambridge University Press
www.cambridge.org/elt

Cambridge Assessment English
www.cambridgeenglish.org

Information on this title:
www.cambridge.org/9781108673013

First published 2020

20 19 18 17 16 15 14 13 12 11 10 9 8 7

Printed in Malaysia by Vivar Printing

A catalogue record for this publication is available from the British Library

ISBN 978-1-108-67301-3 Student's Book and Home Booklet with Online Activities

Author acknowledgements

The author would like to thank the marvellous CUP editing team for their expertise and to Matthew, Ata and mum for everything else.

Publisher acknowledgements

The authors and publishers are grateful to Robert Hill for reviewing the content and style of the stories.

Acknowledgements

The authors and publishers acknowledge the following sources of copyright material and are grateful for the permissions granted. While every effort has been made, it has not always been possible to identify the sources of all the material used, or to trace all copyright holders. If any omissions are brought to our notice, we will be happy to include the appropriate acknowledgements on reprinting and in the next update to the digital edition, as applicable.

Key: BG = Background

Photography

The following photographs are sourced from Getty Images.

BG: Chris Clor; Mima Foto/EyeEm; Marka/Universal Images Group; Elisabeth David/EyeEm; **Reading:** Marc Romanelli; kupicoo/E+; Wavebreakmedia/iStock/Getty Images Plus; Abhishek Thakur/EyeEm; Compassionate Eye Foundation/Rob Daly/OJO Images Ltd/Photodisc; Glow Images; Shin Taro/Moment; JGI/Jamie Grill; Jamie Grill; spxChrome/E+; **Listening:** JohnnyGreig/E+; Gearstd/iStock/Getty Images Plus; FatCamera/E+; karandaev/iStock; imagestock/E+; Studio Omg/EyeEm; Enes Evren/iStock/Getty Image Plus; Chris White/iStock/Getty Images Plus; Martin Jacobs/Photolibrary/Getty Images Plus; **Writing:** GraphicaArtis/Archive Photos; DEA/G. DAGLI ORTI; Universal History Archive/Universal Images Group; Photo 12/Universal Images Group; twpixels/iStock/Getty Images Plus; Kikovic/iStock/Getty Images Plus; Gary Ombler and Andy Crawford/Dorling Kindersley; Creative Crop/DigitalVision; kupicoo/E+; JGI/Jamie Grill; Maskot; Â© Hiya Images/Corbis; PeopleImages/iStock/Getty Images Plus; Rawpixel/iStock/Getty Images Plus; Steve Debenport/E+; kiankhoon/iStock/Getty Images Plus; Gregoria Gregoriou Crowe fine art and creative photography./Moment; **Speaking:** Mike Powell/Photodisc; PhotoAlto/Sigrid Olsson/PhotoAlto Agency RF Collections; Abhishek Thakur/EyeEm; Colin Hawkins/Cultura; Best View Stock; gpointstudio/iStock/Getty Images Plus; Charriau Pierre/The Image Bank; roevin/Moment; Sergei Malgavko/TASS; Stephen Knowles Photography/Moment; Westend61; Floresco Productions/Cultura; **A rainbow visit:** Louis Turner/Stockbyte; Larry Washburn; **What Bobbie likes:** Yevgen Romanenko/Moment; **Piper's favourite food:** Kemi H Photography/Moment Open; **Detective Leon wants a new home!:** romana chapman/Moment; sl-f/iStock/Getty Images Plus; Ed Freeman/Stone; David Santiago Garcia/Aurora; Ed Freeman/Stone.

The following photograph are sourced from other libraries/sources.

Writing: Keith Haring artwork and writing © Keith Haring Foundation; Olga Vorobeva/Alamy Stock Photo.

Front cover photography and illustrations by Amanda Enright; Leo Trinidad; Jhonny Nunez; Pol Cunyat; Benedetta Capriotti; Dan Widdowson; P and P Studio/Shutterstock; Piotr Urakau/Shutterstock.

Audio

Audio production by DN and AE Strauss Ltd, with engineer Mike Dentith.

Design

Design and typeset by Wild Apple Design Ltd
Cover design by Collaborate agency.

Contents

Pre A1 Starters

Listening: words and colours

1 002 **Listen, look and point.**

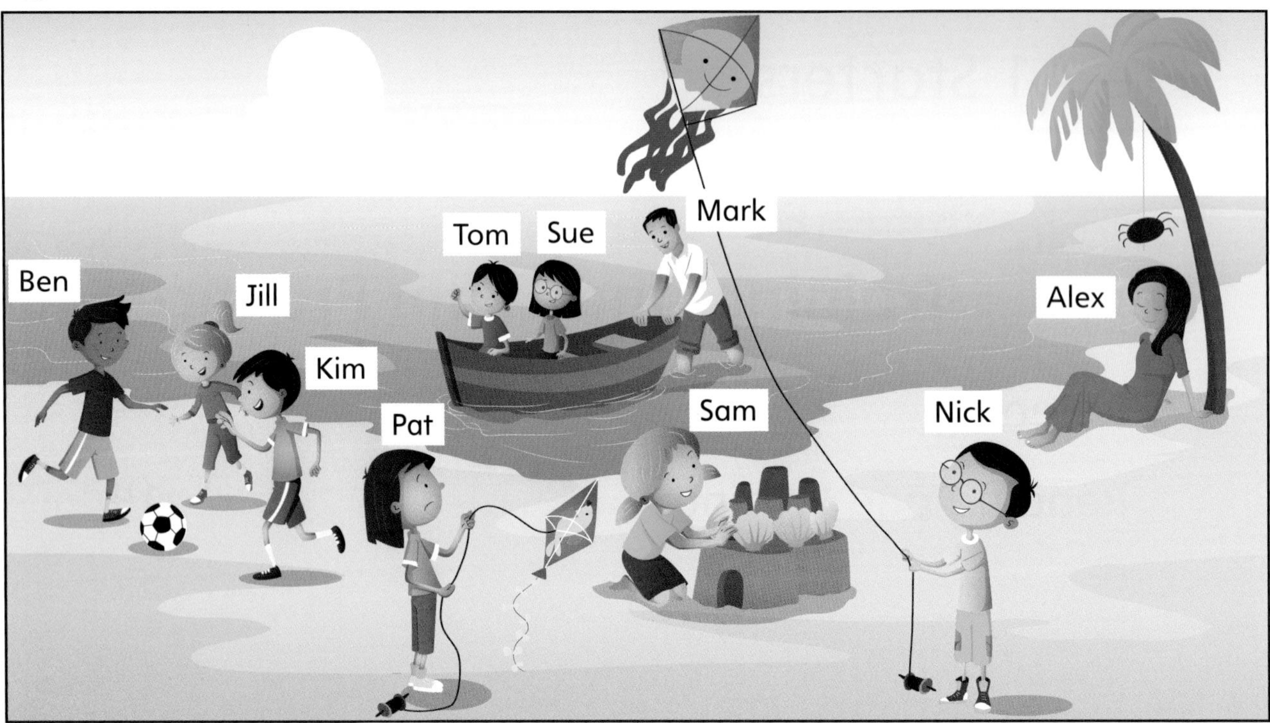

Grammar: simple verb forms

2 In pairs, draw lines to make sentences. There is an example (0).

0 Sam is playing	a a fish on it.
1 Mark has got	b playing football.
2 Sue and Tom are	c in their dad's boat.
3 Alex is wearing	d with the sand.
4 Pat's kite has got	e a small boat.
5 Ben, Kim and Jill are	f a long dress.

TIP! Say what you can see in the picture. This will help you in the test.

Grammar: prepositions

3 Look at the picture. Students A read sentences 1–4 to your partner. Student B look at the picture, is it True or False?

0 Student A: Tom and Sue are in a boat. Student B: True!

1 Jill is wearing a pink T-shirt.

2 Kim is sitting under the tree.

3 Mark has grey hair.

4 Nick is wearing glasses.

Part 1

– 5 questions –

003 **Listen and draw lines. There is one example.**

Alice Matt Dan Eva

May Hugo Grace

Vocabulary: numbers and colours

1 Look, say and point.

3 7 13 11 15 14 20 16 4

Vocabulary: spelling names

2 Look and colour the names.

~~Alice~~	Lucy
Anna	Mark
Bill	~~Matt~~
Dan	Nick
Eva	Sam
Grace	Tom

V	P	F	T	U	D	M	Z	N	A
M	A	Y	Y	B	L	Y	R	D	N
N	T	S	B	E	A	M	S	G	N
F	D	H	Y	M	B	A	A	G	A
M	A	T	T	H	J	W	M	Z	L
L	U	C	Y	C	I	M	O	J	I
D	A	N	N	I	L	A	I	R	C
T	M	B	I	L	L	R	X	Z	E
G	R	A	C	E	I	K	J	W	V
F	V	S	K	X	G	T	O	M	A

3 004 Listen and write the names.

0 Anna

1 ______________

2 ______________

3 ______________

4 ______________

TIP! You can say *cousin* for boys and girls.

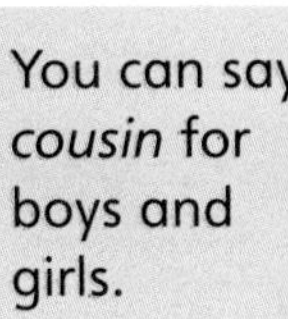

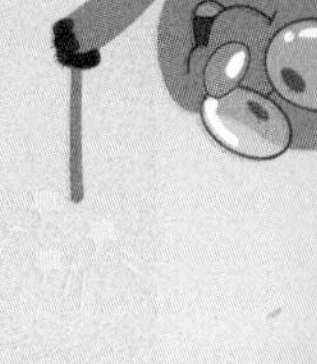

4 Look and read aloud in pairs. Then ask and answer questions about children in your family.

How old are you? I'm 8.

Have you got a sister? Yes, I've got a big sister. She's 14.

How old are you? I'm 7.

Have you got a cousin? Yes, I have. He's 1. He's a baby!

Part 2

– 5 questions –

005 **Read the question. Listen and write a name or number. There are two examples.**

Examples

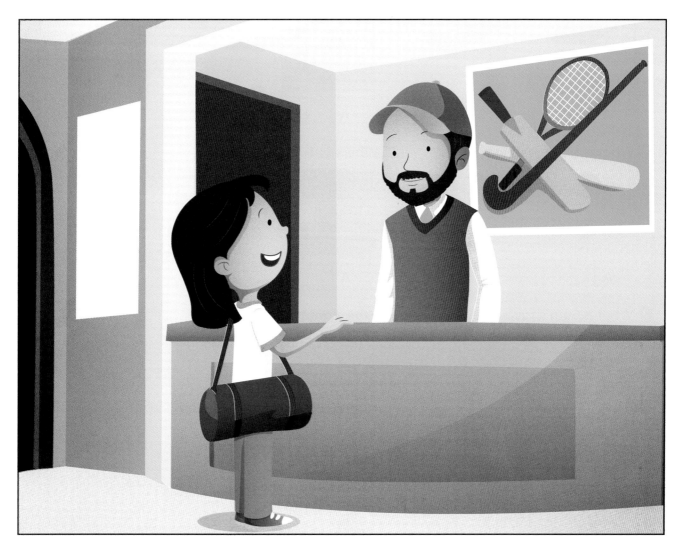

What is the girl's name? Alex

How old is the girl? 7

Questions

1 What is Alex's family name? ____________

2 Where does Alex live? in ____________ Street

3 What number is Alex's house? ____________

4 What colour is Alex's sports skirt? ____________

5 What's the badminton teacher's name? ____________

Listening for information

1 006 **Listen and tick (✓) the correct box. There is one example.**

TIP! Read the questions, look at the pictures and say what you can see. Then listen and choose the right answer.

0 *Which is Anna's helicopter?*

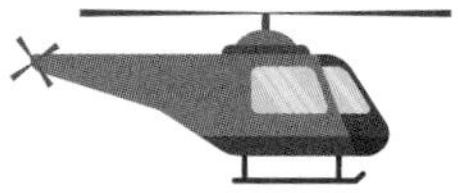

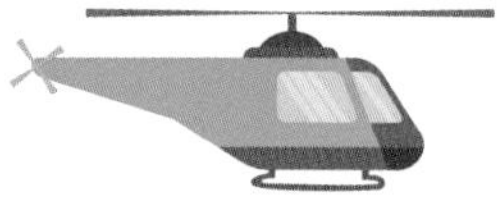

A ☐ B ☑

1 What is Mark wearing?

A ☐ B ☐

2 What is Sam's favourite ice cream?

A ☐ B ☐

3 Which sport are Dan and May doing?

A ☐ B ☐

4 Where is Tom's teddy bear?

A ☐ B ☐

5 Which animal is on the TV?

A ☐ B ☐

2 Look at the pictures. Say what you can see. Now, read and put a tick (✓) or a cross (✗) in the box. There are two examples.

0 *Jellyfish are pink.* ✓

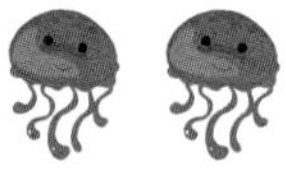

The toy elephant is yellow. ✗

1 The bear is waving. ☐

BEAR

2 The giraffe is eating an ice cream. ☐

3 My baby cousin has got brown hair. ☐

4 My grandma has got a bike. ☐

Listening: choosing the correct picture

3 007 **Listen to the boy and girl and tick (✔) the correct pictures.**

TIP! Listen carefully for 'no' answers, like 'No, it can't.'

0 This is Pat's ...

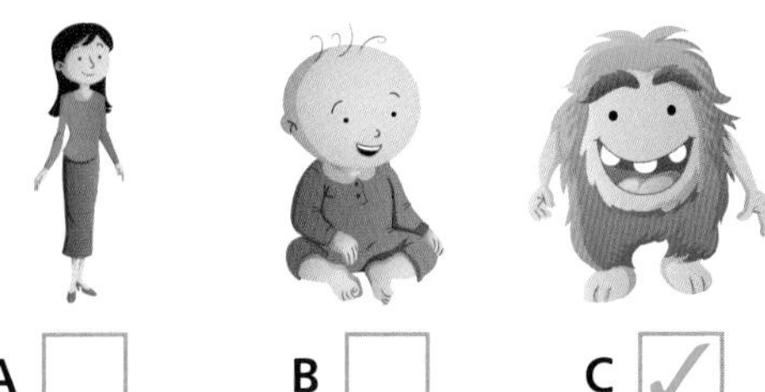

A ☐ B ☐ C ✔

1 It has got a ...

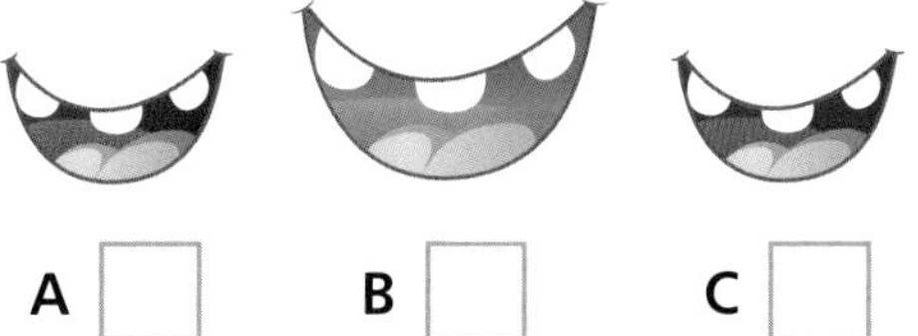

A ☐ B ☐ C ☐

2 It likes eating ...

A ☐ B ☐ C ☐

3 It's wearing ...

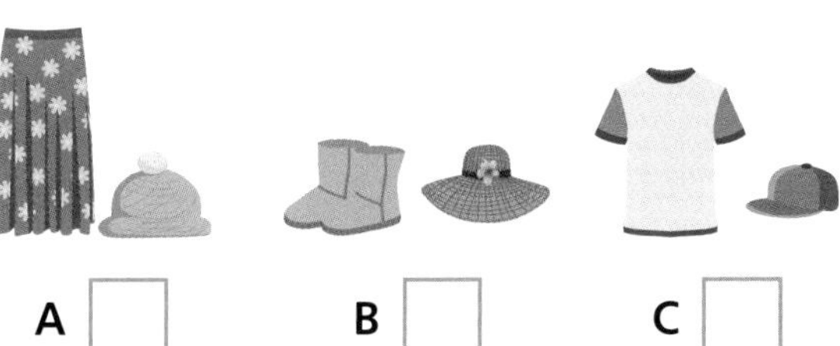

A ☐ B ☐ C ☐

4 It can ...

A ☐ B ☐ C ☐

5 It can ...

A ☐ B ☐ C ☐

TIP! Use 'yes' and 'no' sentences to test your classmates. Have fun!

Get ready!

4 Write two questions. Draw three pictures for each question. Write two short conversations in your notebooks.

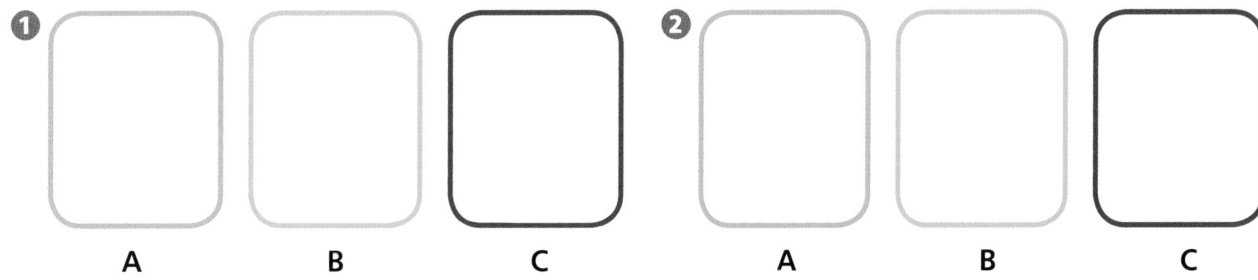

1 A B C 2 A B C

Now, read your conversations about your pictures. Can your classmates choose the correct one?

Part 3

– 5 questions –

 **Listen and tick (✓) the box. There is one example.**

Which car is Jill's grandpa's?

A ☐ B ☐ C ☑

1 Which is Hugo's favourite sport?

A ☐ B ☐ C ☐

2 What's Alice's dad cooking?

A ☐ B ☐ C ☐

3 Which animal is in the bath?

A ☐ B ☐ C ☐

4 Where are Alex's shorts?

A ☐ B ☐ C ☐

5 Which ship is Kim's?

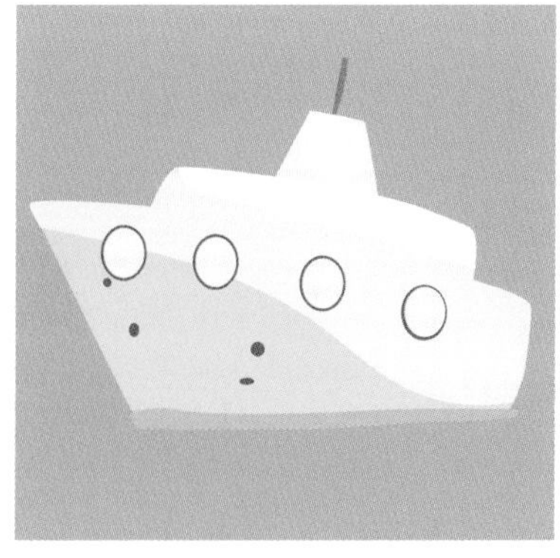

A ☐ B ☐ C ☐

Vocabulary: colours

1 009 **Listen and tick (✓) the correct answer.**

0

A ✓ B ☐ C ☐

2

A ☐ B ☐ C ☐

1

A ☐ B ☐ C ☐

3

A ☐ B ☐ C ☐

Vocabulary: prepositions

2 010 **Where is the frog? Listen and write the numbers in order.**

A  1

B  ___

C  ___

D  ___

E  ___

F  ___

G  ___

TIP! In Part 4, learn how to say where things are with prepositions. When do we say *in*, *on*, *in front of* or *next to*, *between*, *behind* and *under*?

Get ready!

3 011 **Listen and colour. In pairs write about the teddy bears.**

0 *The yellow teddy bear is in the boy's bag.*

1 ______________________________

2 ______________________________

Part 4

– 5 questions –

012 **Listen and colour. There is one example.**

Vocabulary: matching

1 Match the sentences and the pictures.

A 

B 

C 

D 

E 

F 

0 These are pencils. ___C___
1 This is a frog. ______
2 These are balls. ______
3 This is a camera. ______
4 These are sweets. ______
5 This is a coconut. ______

TIP! Look at the sentences and decide if they are about one or more things. Remember! *This is a* = 1 thing, *These are* = more things.

TIP! We usually put an *s* or *es* at the end of a plural word, but we say *two fish* and *two sheep*.

Grammar: singular and plural

2 Choose the correct word.

0 **This is a / These are** balloons.
1 **This is a / These are** baseball cap.
2 **This is a / These are** sausages.
3 **This is a / These are** tennis racket.
4 **This is a / These are** zebra.
5 **This is a / These are** jeans.

Reading: understanding sentences

3 Read the sentences. Draw two correct pictures and three wrong pictures.

0 These are fish. ✓

1 This is a chicken. ✓

2 This is a house. ✗

3 These are boots. ✓

4 This is an elephant. ✗

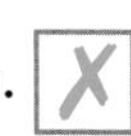

5 These are watches. ✗

Part 1

– 5 questions –

Look and read. Put a tick (✓) or a cross (✗) in the box.
There are two examples.

Examples

This is a potato. ✓

These are shoes. ✗

1 This is a skateboard. ☐

2 This is a rug. ☐

3 These are watermelons. ☐

4 This is a board game. ☐

5 This is a jellyfish. ☐

Reading: sentences about a picture

1 Read the sentences and choose the correct answer. Why are the other two answers wrong?

0 The boy and girl are in the **bookshop / park / street.** (street circled)

1 The woman with black hair is **drawing / driving on / crossing** the street.

2 The man in the fruit shop has got **pink / grey / brown** hair.

3 There's a **giraffe / hippo / cow** in the car.

4 The children are wearing **hats / shorts / jeans**.

5 The girl is holding a **lorry / skateboard / motorbike**.

6 You can see two **tigers / sheep / horses** in the picture.

Grammar: talking about the present

2 Look at the picture. Read the sentences and put a tick (✓) or a cross (✗).

0 There is a jellyfish in the clothes shop. ✓

1 It's wearing sunglasses. ☐

2 The jellyfish has got green hair ☐

3 It's sitting on a chair. ☐

4 The T-shirt has got a picture of a beach on it. ☐

5 The jellyfish is sad. ☐

3 Write 3 more sentences about the picture, one 'yes' and two 'no'.

1 ______________________ Yes

2 ______________________ No

3 ______________________ No

Part 2

– 5 questions –

Look and read. Write *yes* or *no*.

Examples

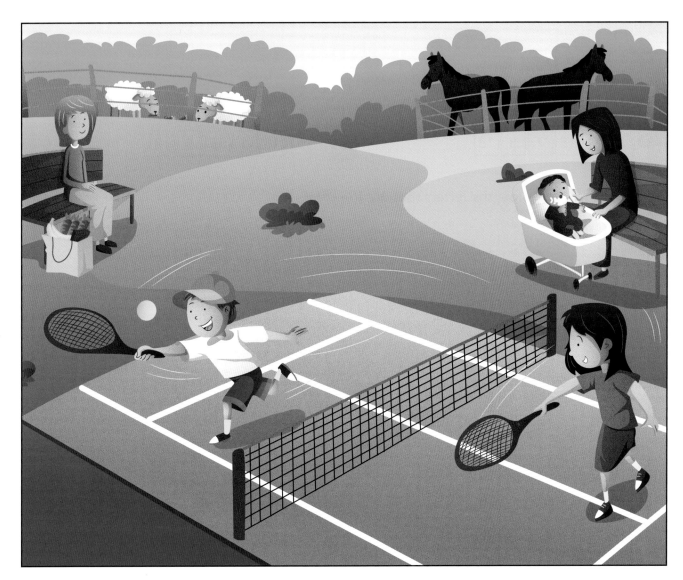

The people are having fun in the park. *yes*

The boy is watching television. *no*

Questions

1. The boy and girl are playing tennis. ______
2. The girl has got black hair. ______
3. The baby is eating ice cream. ______
4. The woman's bag is closed. ______
5. The horses are drinking some water. ______

Vocabulary: spelling

1 Look at the letters and numbers. Look at the code words. What are they? In pairs draw and write code words.

A	B	C	D	E	F	G	H	I	J	K	L	M	N	O	P	Q	R	S	T	U	V	W	X	Y	Z
1	2	3	4	5	6	7	8	9	10	11	12	13	14	15	16	17	18	19	20	21	22	23	24	25	26

0 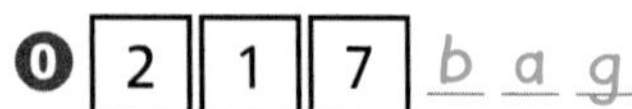 2 1 7 b a g

1 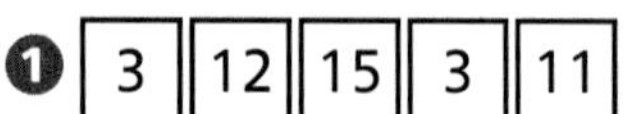 3 12 15 3 11 _ _ _ _ _ 

3 13 15 21 19 5 _ _ _ _ _ 

2 2 21 18 7 5 18 _ _ _ _ _ _

4 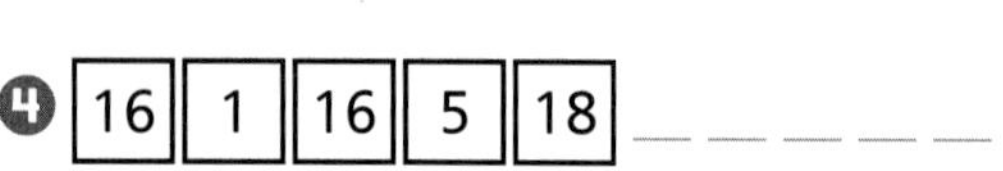 16 1 16 5 18 _ _ _ _ _

2 Write the words. Colour the letters that are the same.

0 cool	door	floor	o o is the same
1 socks	tennis racket	jacket	_ _ is the same
2 mouse	house	trousers	_ _ is the same
3 teacher	computer	flower	_ _ is the same
4 pea	bear	sea	_ _ is the same

Grammar: articles and prepositions

3 Read the sentences. Choose the correct answers.

0 I play **at** / **in** the park every afternoon.
1 I like watching TV in **the** / — bedroom.
2 He is swimming in **a** / **the** sea.
3 Tom is **at** / **in** the kitchen.
4 I play baseball **at** / **in** the weekend.
5 I always eat **an** / **a** ice cream at the beach.

Get ready!

4 Look at the pictures. Then write the words.

0  b a g

1  s _ _ _

2  h _ _

3  j _ _ _ _

4  j _ _ _ _ _

5 d _ _ _ _

6  g _ _ _ _ _ _

7  s _ _ _ _

8  b _ _ _ _

Part 3

– 5 questions –

Look at the pictures. Look at the letters. Write the words.

Example

l i m e

Questions

1

2

3

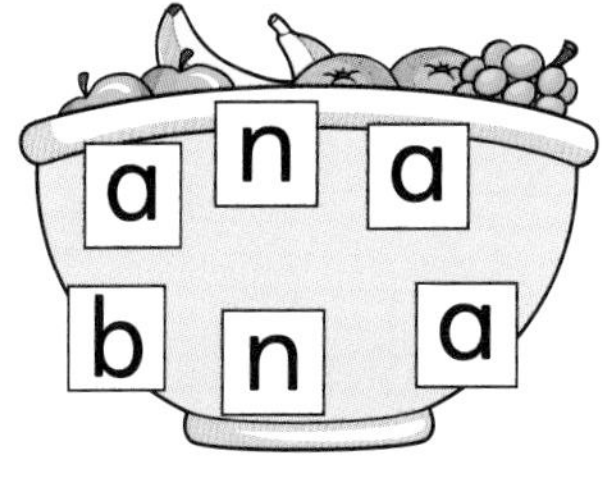

4

5

_ _ _ _ _ _ _ _ _

Vocabulary: spelling

1 Look at the pictures and say the words. Write the words.

0 

c a t

1 

b _ _

2 

l _ _ _

3 

c _ _ _ _ _ _ _ _

4

c _ _ _ _ _ _ _

5 

p _ _ _ _

6 

h _ _ _ _

7 

f _ _ _

Reading: sentences

2 Read and cross out the wrong word.

0 Fish have **tails** / ~~**legs**~~.

1 A cat can run and jump on its **arms** / **legs**.

2 Many birds sleep in **trees** / **flats**.

3 We eat lunch in the **dining room** / **bathroom**.

4 He is wearing a baseball **cap** / **jacket** on his head.

5 Many horses like eating **apples** / **juice**.

6 I like flying my **bat** / **kite** in the park.

7 I live with my parents and my **teacher** / **grandma**.

TIP! In Part 4, choose the words that go best in the sentences. Don't write silly sentences in the test!

Writing the missing words in a text

3 Read the text about bears. Write the correct word to complete the sentences.

Bears

Bears are big **(0)** animals and they can be very scary. Many bears are black or brown but some are white, like polar bears. Some bears can swim in water and catch **(1)** ________ in their **(2)** ________. Some bears eat **(3)** ________ from small animals and some eat parts of trees. Many bears have a big head, a long body and a short **(4)** ________ at the end of its body. A bear can run fast on its four **(5)** ________. Some bears sleep in trees and you can see them in zoos.

animals

fish

tail

meat

eyes

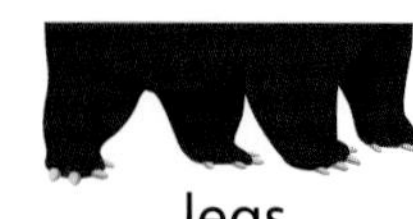

legs

mouth

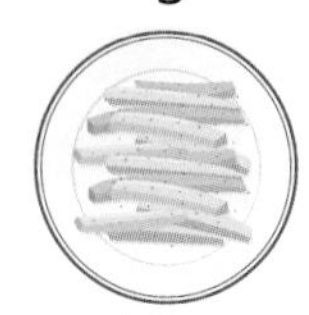

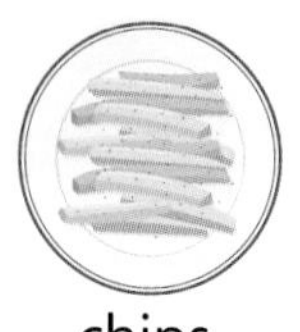

chips

Part 4

– 5 questions –

Read this. Choose a word from the box. Write the correct word next to numbers 1–5. There is one example.

Our playground

We have a big playground at my ___school___. It is outside my (**1**) ______________ and it has got a big tree in it. We sit under the tree and the (**2**) ______________ reads us a story from a big (**3**) ______________ at the end of the day. We eat (**4**) ______________ in a big room next to the playground, then we play (**5**) ______________ there. I love our playground – it's cool!

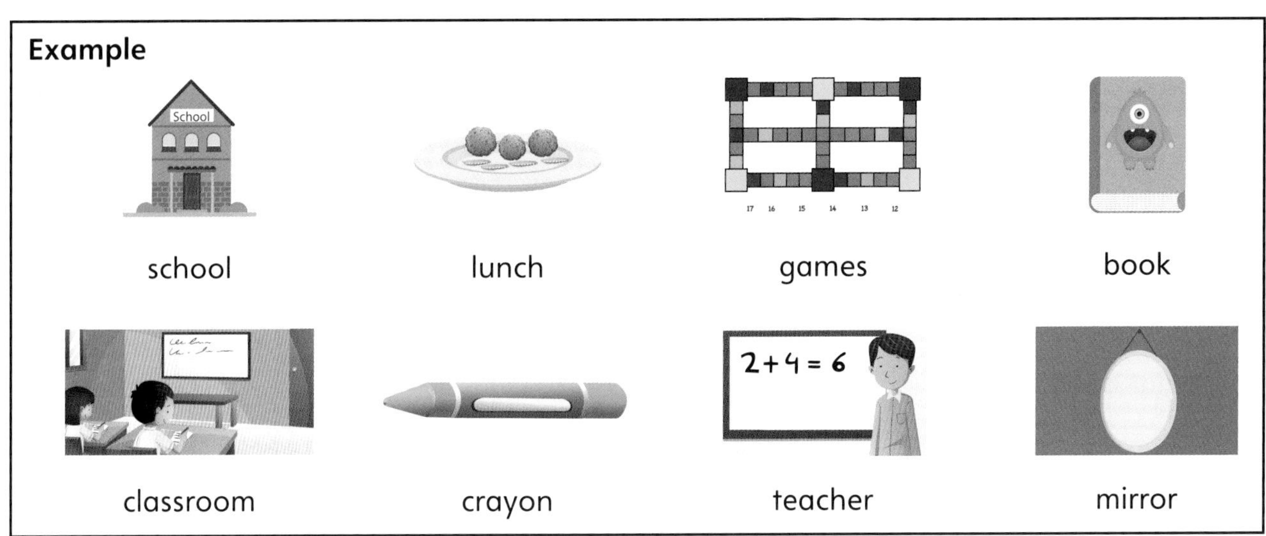

Vocabulary

1 Look at the pictures. Write three words about what you can see in each picture.

1 ______
______
______

2 ______
______
______

3 ______
______
______

TIP! In Part 5, you only have to write one-word answers. Before you read the questions, look at the pictures and say what you can see in the pictures.

TIP! The questions in Part 5 are usually '*What is/are the … doing? What has the … got? Where is/are the …? Who is …ing?* and *How many …?* Practise asking and answering these questions when you see story pictures.

Asking and answering questions

2 Read the questions. The answers are wrong! Make the answers right.

Where are the people? in the ~~playground~~ park

What are they doing? ~~flying~~ walking

1 How many animals can you see? ~~twelve~~ ______

2 What does the cat want to do? eat the ~~dog~~ ______

3 What is the dog doing? ~~sleeping~~ ______ in the water

4 What is the girl doing? ~~catching~~ ______ a ball

5 Where is the ball? in the dog's ~~nose~~ ______

6 Who is not happy? the ~~baby duck~~ ______

Storytelling

3 Read the questions and say the answers. Then tell the story in groups of three.

Picture 1

Where are the people?
What are they wearing?
What animals can you see?
What does the cat want to do?
What does the dog want to do?

Picture 2

What is the cat doing?
What is the dog doing?
Who is saying 'Oh no!'? Why?
What is the girl throwing?
What is the woman doing?

Picture 3

Where is the ball now?
What is sitting on the dog's head?
Which animals are clapping?
What are the people doing?
Who is happy? Why?
Who isn't happy? Why?

Get ready!

4 In pairs, think of a story! Draw three pictures. Write two questions for each picture and show them to your classmates. Can they answer the questions?

TIP! Learning how to tell stories will help you answer the story questions in Part 5.

Part 5

– 5 questions –

Look at the pictures and read the questions.
Write one-word answers.

Examples

Where are the boy and girl? in the living room

How many lizards are there? three

Questions

1 Who is playing with the lizards? the ______

2 What colour is the lizard now? green and ____________________

3 What is the lizard doing? ____________________ up the wall

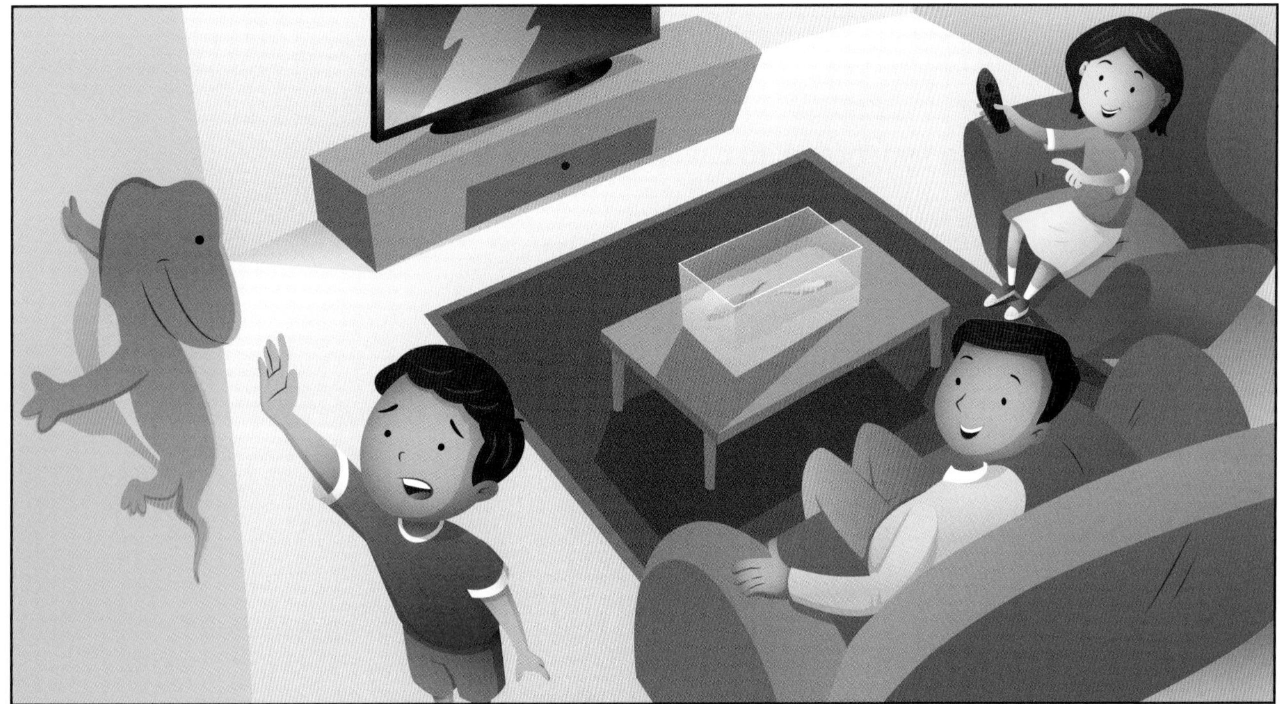

4 Who is trying to catch the lizard? the ____________________

5 What is the man doing? sitting on the ____________________

Objects in a picture

1 Look at the picture. Write words in the clouds. Then say the words and point.

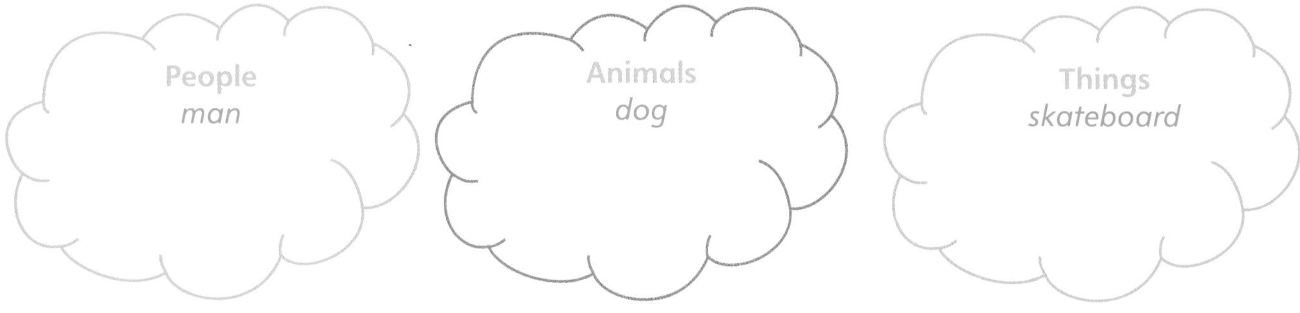

Describing where things are

2 Read and complete the sentences with a word or phrase from the box.

behind   between   in   in front of   next to   ~~on~~

0 The dog is ___on___ the skateboard.

1 The boy is ________ the elephant.

2 The giraffe is ________ the zebra.

3 The monkeys are ________ the tree.

4 The zebra is ________ the elephant and the giraffe.

5 The tree is ________ the house.

SCENE PICTURE

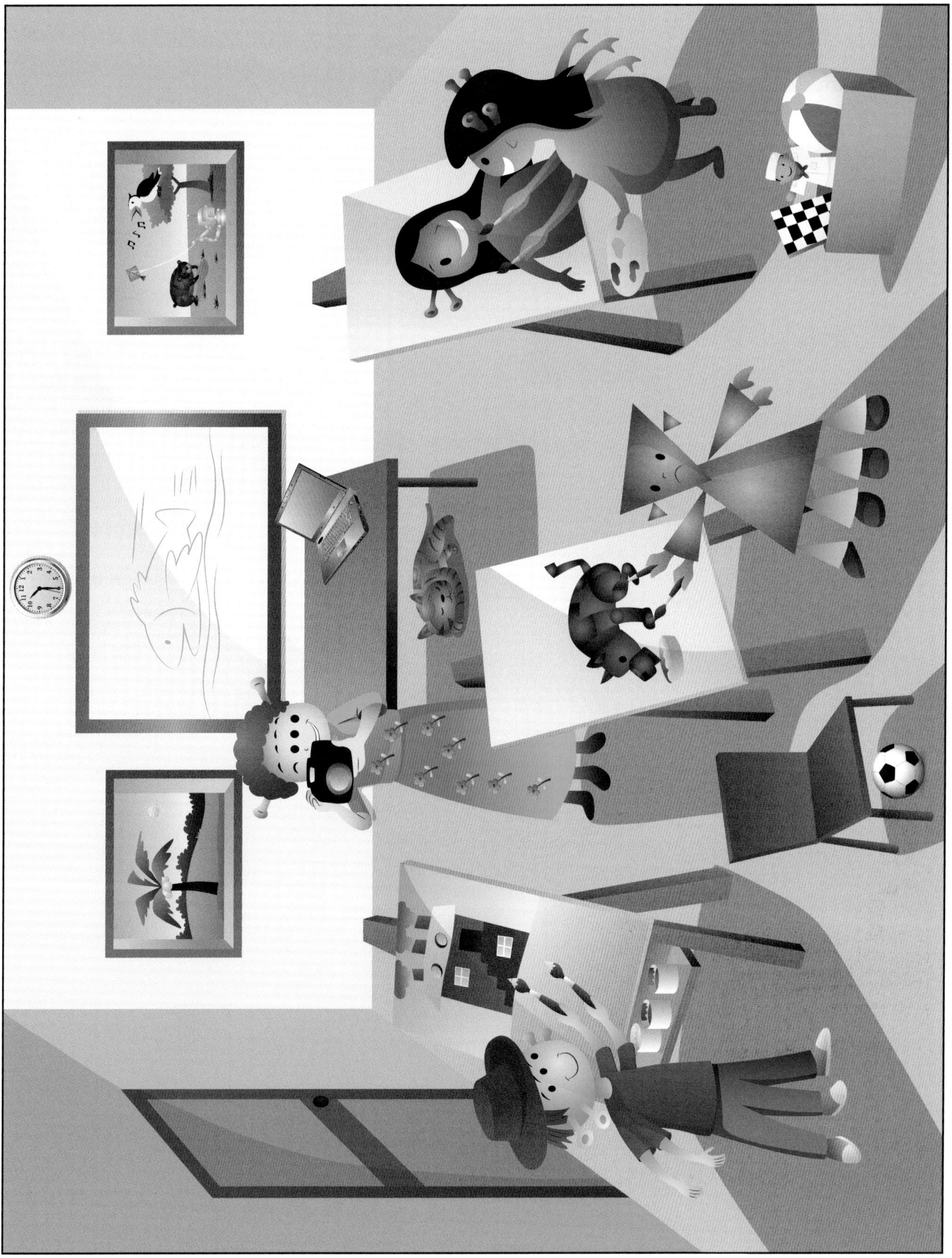

1 Look at the pictures. Talk about each picture in pairs.
What colour are the things in the pictures?
Which things do you have?
Which things do you like? Why?

1 
rubber

2 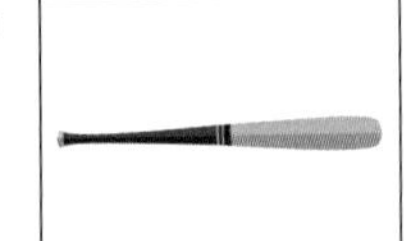
bat

3 
sheep

4 
bag

5 
chicken

6 
TV

7 

bike

8 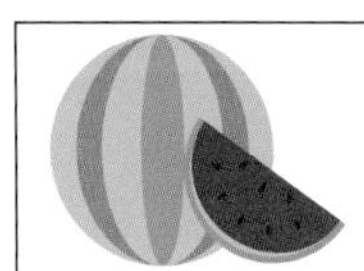
watermelon

2 Ask and answer the questions in pairs.

TIP! Try to give answers of more than one word.

About you

How old are you?
How many brothers or sisters have you got?

About your free time

Which toys do you play with?
Where do you play?

About your teacher

What's your teacher's name?
Has he/she got brown hair/green eyes?

OBJECT CARDS

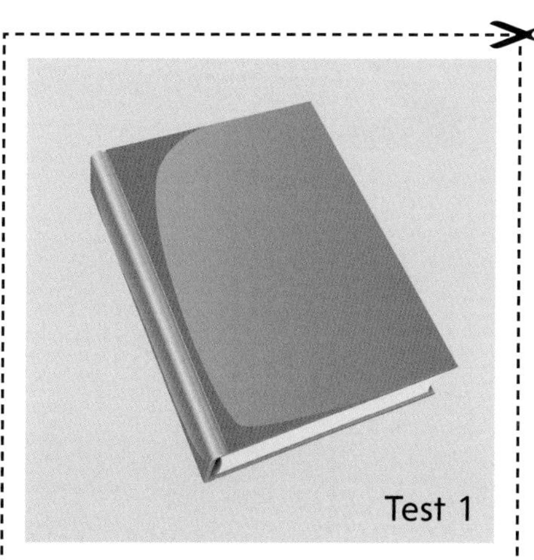

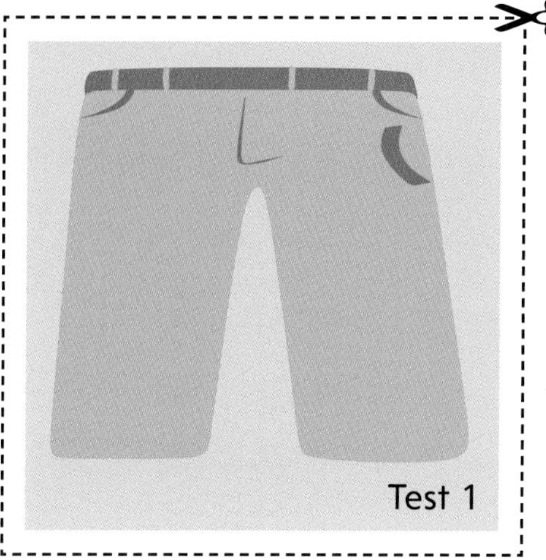

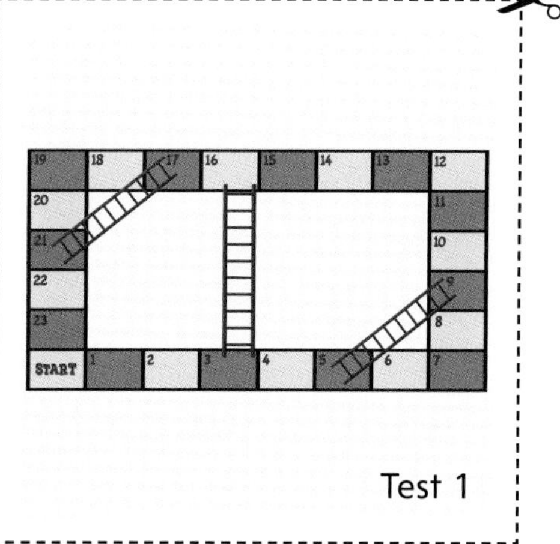

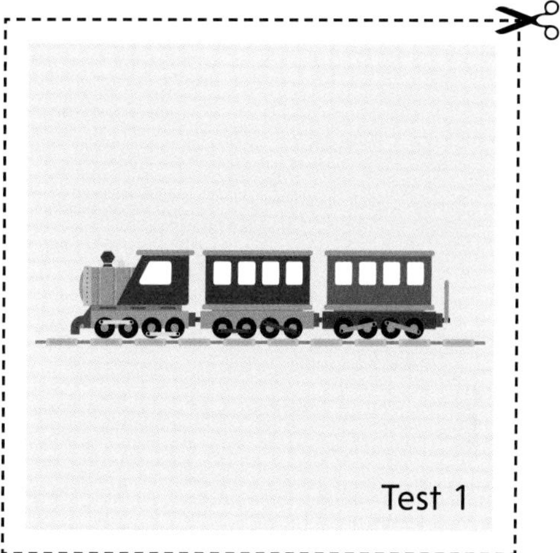

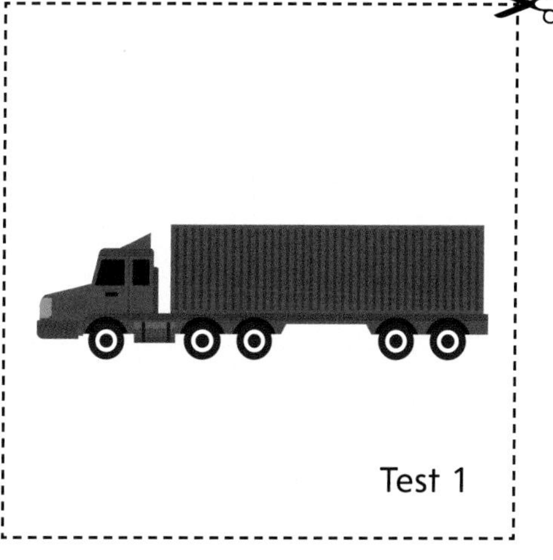

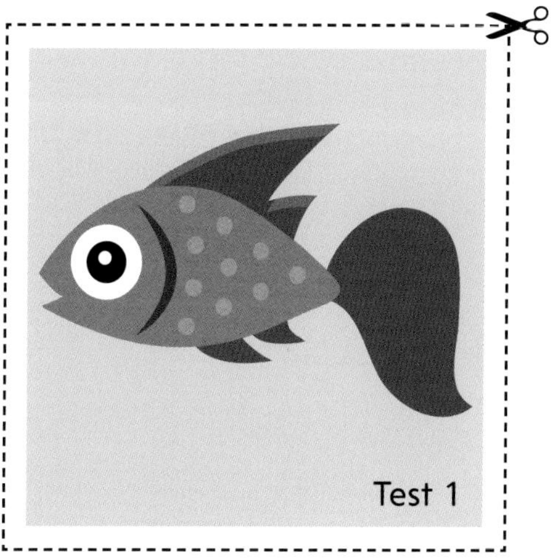

Test 2

Part 1

– 5 questions –

013 **Listen and draw lines. There is one example.**

Lucy Hugo May Nick

Eva Dan Grace

Part 2

– 5 questions –

014 **Read the question. Listen and write a name or a number.**
There are two examples.

Examples

What is the boy's name?	Tom
How old is he?	8

Questions

1. How many lizards are in Tom's box? ____________

2. What is the green lizard's name? Mr ____________

3. How many grapes do the lizards eat in the morning? ____________

4. What is the number of Tom's flat? ____________

5. Where does Tom live? in ____________ Street

Part 3

– 5 questions –

015 **Listen and tick (✓) the box. There is one example.**

Which animal is Alice drawing?

A ☐

B ✓

C ☐

1 Where is Ben's robot?

A ☐

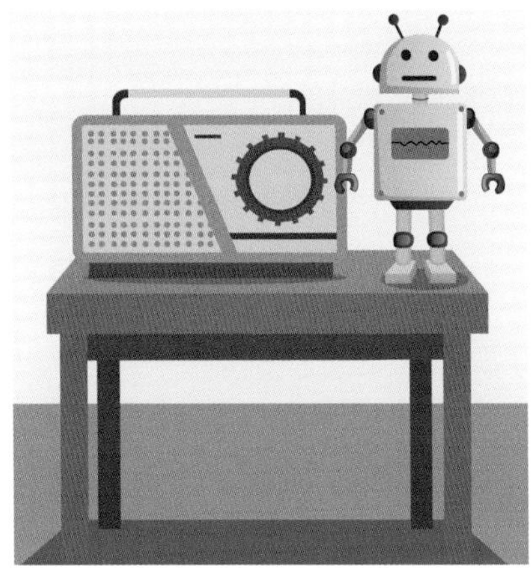

B ☐

C ☐

2 Which is Sue's favourite fruit?

A ☐

B ☐

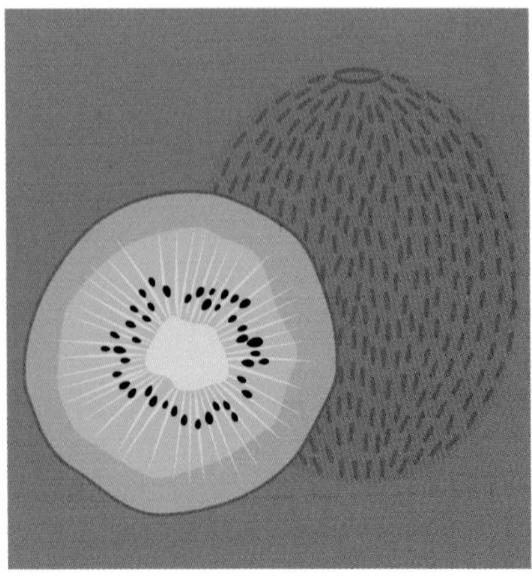

C ☐

3 What is Sam doing now?

A ☐

B ☐

C ☐

4 What can the family have for dinner?

A ☐

B ☐

C ☐

5 Which sport is Pat learning about today?

A ☐

B ☐

C ☐

Part 4

– 5 questions –

016 **Listen and colour. There is one example.**

Part 1

– 5 questions –

Look and read. Put a tick (✔) or a cross (✗) in the box.

There are two examples.

Examples

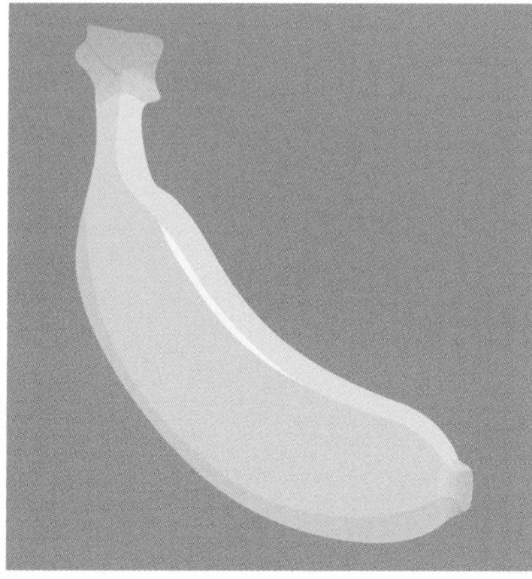

This is a pear. 

These are aliens. 

Questions

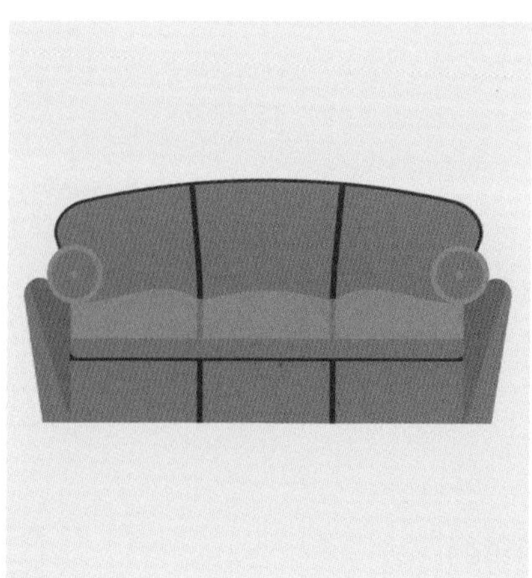

This is a sofa. 

2 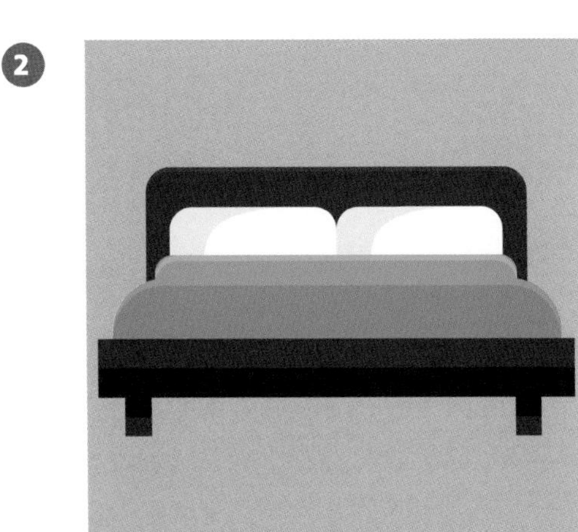

This is a box. ☐

3 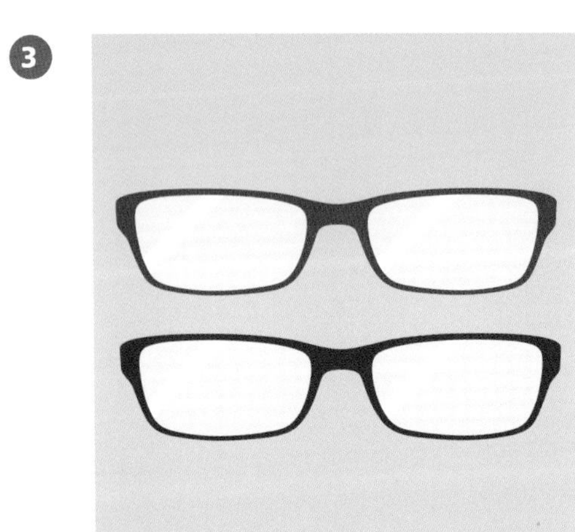

These are glasses. ☐

4 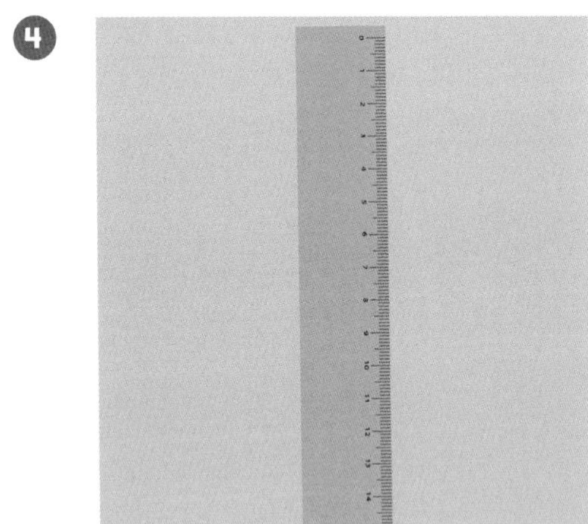

This is a ruler. ☐

5 

These are crocodiles. ☐

Part 2

– 5 questions –

Look and read. Write *yes* or *no*.

Examples

There is a picture of a chicken on the poster. ___*yes*___

The doll is on the table. ___no___

Questions

1. The teacher is writing a word. ______

2. You can see some flowers. ______

3. The girl is picking up a book. ______

4. One of the boys has brown hair. ______

5. The doors of the cupboard are open. ______

Part 3

– 5 questions –

Look at the pictures. Look at the letters. Write the words.

Example

b u s

Questions

_ _ _

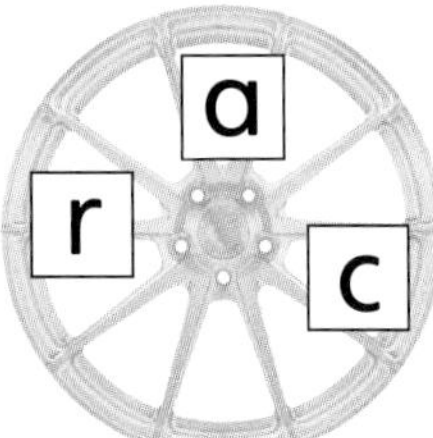

2

_ _ _ _

3

_ _ _ _ _

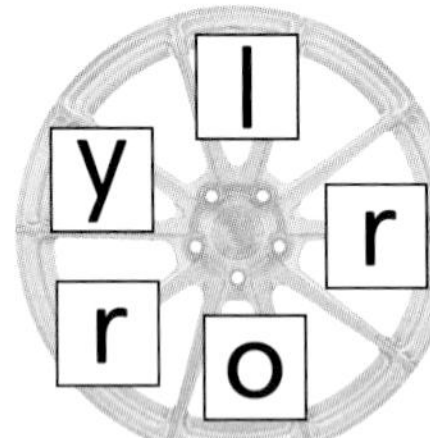

4

_ _ _ _ _

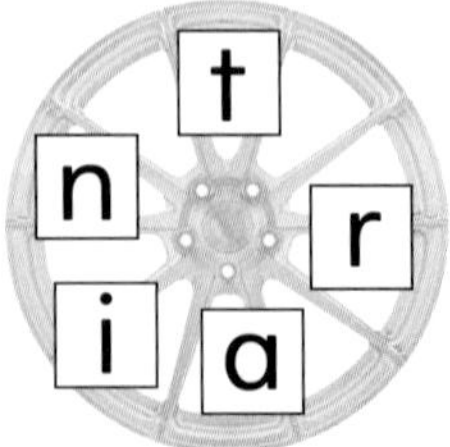

5

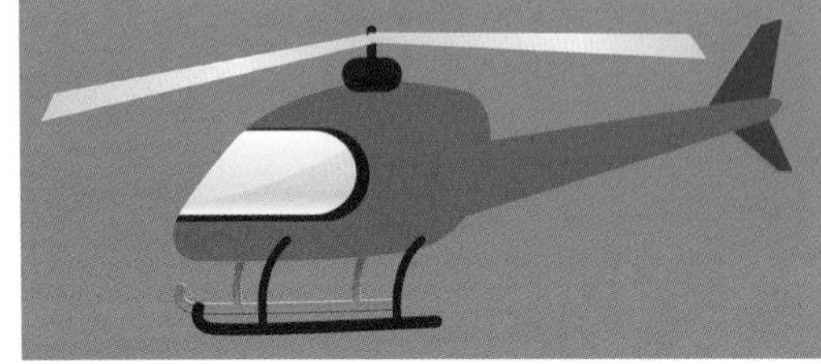

_ _ _ _ _ _ _ _ _ _

Part 4

– 5 questions –

Read this. Choose a word from the box. Write the correct word next to numbers 1–5. There is one example.

Baseball

Tom's favourite ___sport___ is baseball. He loves watching baseball

on his tablet or on **(1)** ______________. He plays baseball with his

(2) ______________ from school, too. They can play baseball at the

(3) ______________ or at the beach. Tom throws and catches the

(4) ______________ with his hands. But he hits it with his new

(5) ______________! 'It's fantastic!' he says.

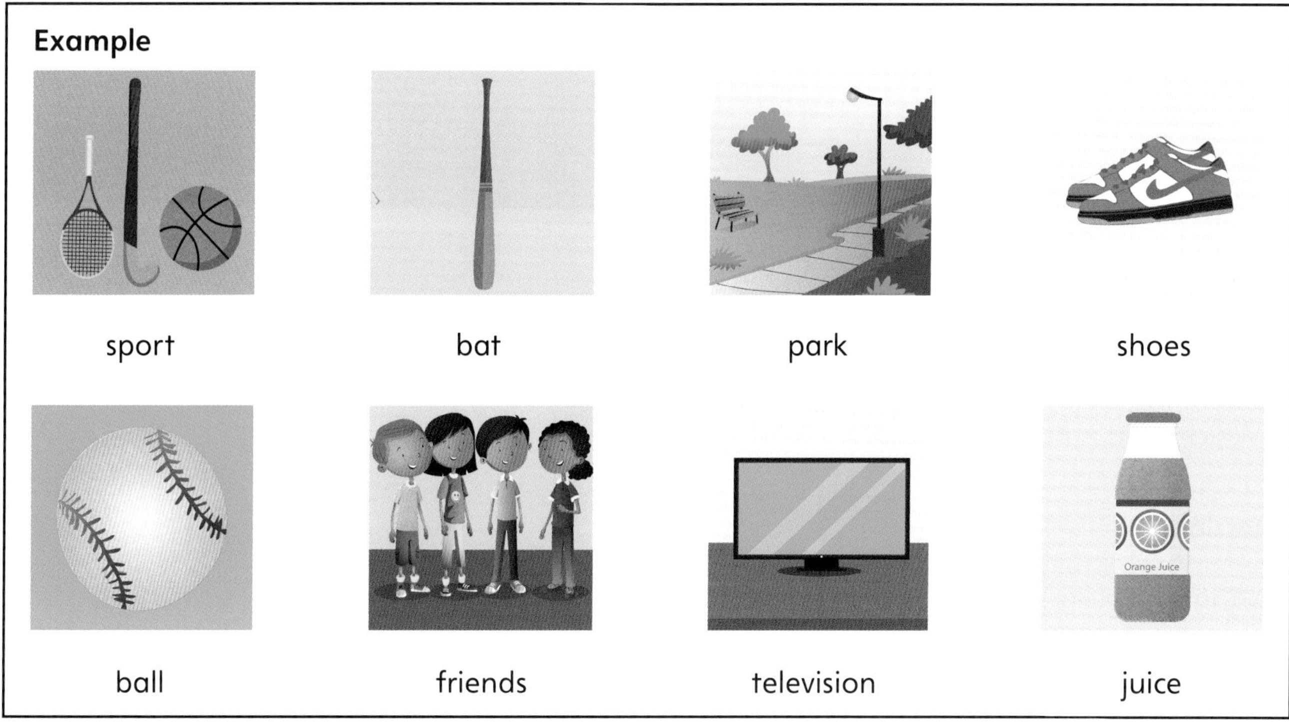

Part 5

– 5 questions –

Look at the pictures and read the questions. Write one-word answers.

Examples

How many children are there? two

Which child is riding the horse? the girl

Questions

1 What is the horse doing? ______

2 Where is the bird? in the ____________

3 What is the horse eating? an ____________

4 Where is the bird now? on the horse's ____________

5 Who is taking the photo? the children's ____________

SCENE PICTURE

Blank Page

OBJECT CARDS

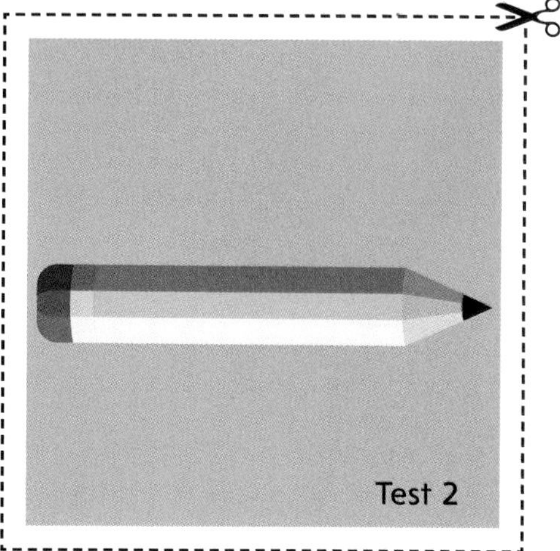

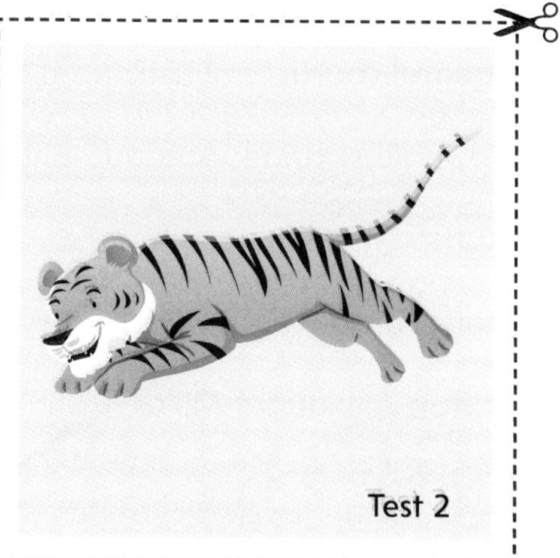

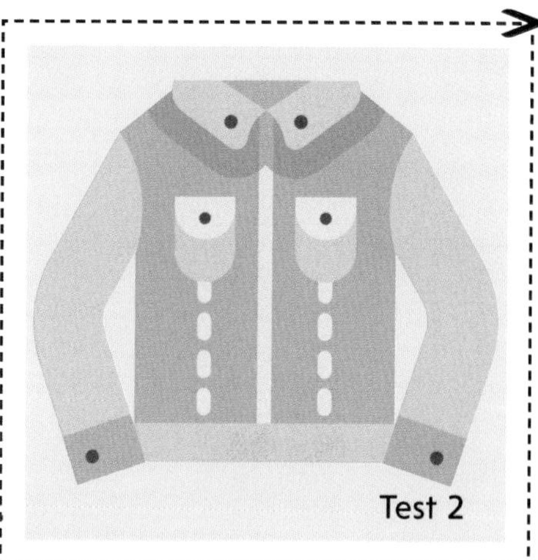

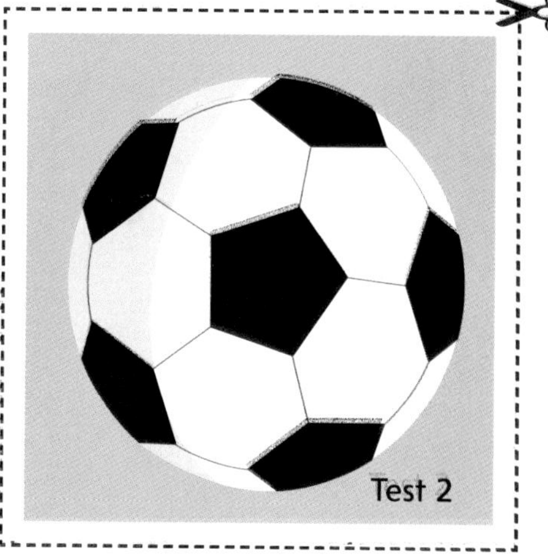

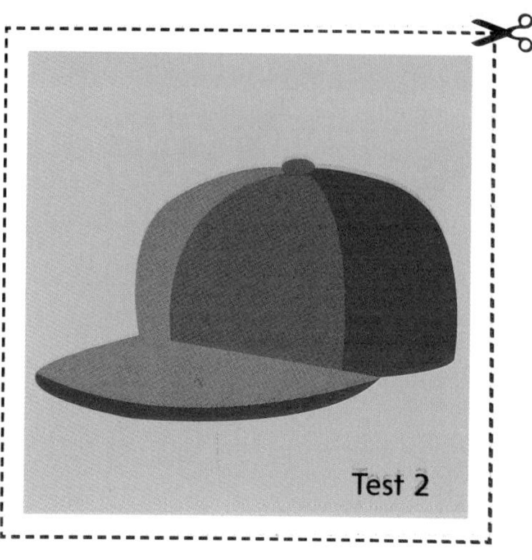

Acknowledgements

The authors and publishers acknowledge the following sources of copyright material and are grateful for the permissions granted. While every effort has been made, it has not always been possible to identify the sources of all the material used, or to trace all copyright holders. If any omissions are brought to our notice, we will be happy to include the appropriate acknowledgements on reprinting and in the next update to the digital edition, as applicable.

The authors and publishers would like to thank the following contributors:

Page make up, illustration and animations: QBS Learning

Squirrel character illustration: Leo Trinidad

Cover illustration: Amanda Enright

Author: Trish Burrow

Audio production: DN and AE Strauss Ltd and James Miller

Editor: Alexandra Miller

Pre A1 Starters Trainer

Two practice tests without answers

1

Cambridge University Press
www.cambridge.org/elt

Cambridge Assessment English
www.cambridgeenglish.org

Information on this title: www.cambridge.org/9781108564304

First published 2019

40 39 38 37 36 35 34 33 32 31 30 29 28 27 26 25 24 23

Printed in Malaysia by Vivar Printing

A catalogue record for this publication is available from the British Library

ISBN 978-1-108-56430-4 Pre A1 Starters Mini Trainer with Audio Download